God goes to College too

Volume 2

BIBLICAL PRINCIPLES FOR NAVIGATING THE COLLEGE EXPERIENCE

KAYON RODNEY

Copyright

ISBN: 978-1-954755-34-5

Published by:
Restoration of the Breach without Borders
West Palm Beach, Florida 33407
restorativeauthor@gmail.com
Tele: (561) 388-2949

Formatting and Publishing done by:
Sherene Morrison
Publisher.20@aol.com

Unless otherwise stated Scripture verses are quoted from the King James Version of the Bible.

Foreword

Stop!

Have you read volume one of *God goes to College too*?

If not, I encourage you to make it a priority to do so, even as you delve into the depths of volume two. Though the volumes can be read apart from each other, the wealth of knowledge to be garnered from reading both is unmatched.

Where volume 1 lays the foundation for readers to come to an understanding of self and discover their purpose, volume 2 expands into other areas. Volume 2 focuses on the academic, financial, social and "how to live in the world" topics which are crucial for students navigating the college journey. These are topics which many mainstream Christian communities rarely delve into, whether because of a lack of understanding or because of the taboo associated with them. These include topics such as sex, sexuality and dating.

Kayon dares to go where others fear to venture, spitting straight facts and guidance, seasoned with the love of a parent trying to steer his or her child away from the wrong path and onto the right one. Or, if you're more mature, the conversational tone gives the impression of a more seasoned sibling lovingly providing instructions to a younger one. The method of coaching used in this book is one that is straightforward, topical and practical, giving examples where necessary and provoking one to introspection. The expected result is that readers will be sufficiently equipped with intentional measures they can put in place for maintaining the right course or making a change, of course for the better.

From the in-depth information, advice and strategies, to the language and expressions, it is evident that great care was taken in writing these books. Reading them you can expect to feel as if you are conversing with a wise, longtime friend who has your best interest at heart. Readers will be left equipped with a wealth of spiritual, financial, relational and mental knowledge which are vital for successfully manoeuvring the college journey with God. Through these books, Kayon continues to remind us that in all that we do and say, God should be at the centre and forefront of our minds regardless of the many trials and temptations that plague us.

It is also important to note that though this book is primarily directed at college students, it is not isolated to that group. In fact, it is an invaluable resource for anyone who is desirous of and seeking to live a joyous, fulfilling Christian life. This, ultimately, can be seen as the aim of this book. A book dedicated to helping persons grow in the knowledge, grace, and purpose of our Lord Jesus Christ.

May this book convict, challenge and encourage you in love to strive towards living your life for Christ as it has done for me.

K.A.L. Lloyd (female vice president)
Universities and Colleges Christian Fellowship (UCCF)
UTECH
2022-2023

DEDICATION

To every person who has ever felt inadequate and incapable of accomplishing the task for which they have been called.

Here's to you…

Use what you have been given and entrust the rest to God.

"And the LORD asked him, "What is that in your hand?" "A staff," he replied. "Throw it on the ground," said the LORD. So Moses threw it on the ground…"

Exodus 4:2-3

ACKNOWLEDGEMENTS

This work is the culmination of grace. Lord, thank You for the process and all the persons you have used to help make this second volume a success.

To my husband and daughter, thank you for supporting my endeavours and giving me time and space to complete this work. My "graced for this" reviewer and editor, Dr. Ruth Baker-Gardner: thank you for your, advice, practical assistance and "leading by example" unwavering support. Graced and positioned for such a time as this. I cannot express my thanks enough.

To my publisher, extended, church and school family, friends and acquaintances who supported me in this endeavour in their own unique ways, thank you. This work is a success thanks to the impact or support of every single person that has ever graced my path in life.

Thank you all.

CONTENTS

Introduction

MAXIMIZING YOUR POTENTIAL.
WALKING INTO PURPOSE.

So, here you are!

You've made the big decision to enter College!

Or, in some cases, the big decision has been made for you. Either way, looks like you are heading off to college, or you are already there! With this decision comes excitement, trepidation, elation and a range of other emotions. How will it be? Will I do well? Will I be able to pay the fees? Am I good enough? Will I make it this time around - that is for those who would have tried this or some other form of schooling, but stopped short of completion.

The range of thoughts, emotions and feelings are too many to list. There is one thought, however, that rarely ever gets thrown into the mix, and that is the thought of, "How does this fit in with my purpose? Or, what role will God play on this journey?" Thoughts of God often become a "shut-in-the-box" concept for many persons in college who identify their belief as being Christianity – "practicing" or "professing".

The issue...

This "shut-in-the-box" concept of God comes as the temptations, rigours and demands of college compete fiercely for the time, attention and righteous living which are necessary for maintaining a fruitful relationship with God. Many Christians have gotten caught in the "busyness", time constraints and temptations to compromise while in college, to the detriment of their relationship with God. This of course often results in them only calling upon God when backed into a corner by the challenges of college.

In other words, God gets a chance to come out of the box for "genie-type" prayer requests geared at getting the tuition paid, or for that oh-so-desperately-needed passing grade. After that moment passes, He is once again locked in that box - at least mentally - and pushed to the back of thoughts and actions. Such a big God, OUR BIG GOD, gets reduced to emergencies when there is a need for passing grades and money, (in our minds) based on our actions. This is a great disservice and affront to our awesome and mighty Creator who is limitless and without measure or boundaries. A God who is all-powerful, mighty, and YES... interested in the affairs of His people beyond occasional visits.

Added to the issue of spiritual neglect, there are also several distractions and snares associated with the much fantasized "college experience". By the world's much-touted standards this is the time of freedom to let loose (sexually and otherwise), explore, experiment, party, whatever your soul desires. Add to that the pressures of achieving and fitting in, tight deadlines, opposing views, seeking out scarce resources, socializing with friends - the whole works. Equally, many have bought into the culture of pursuing academic success without necessarily maximizing their potential and pursuing purpose. With all these potential snares, if Christians are not deliberate, strategic and discerning they will quickly find themselves being led by worldly standards in their pursuits, failing to reach their God-given potential and purpose for the season.

Addressing the issue...

Addressing the issue may be covered in these two sentences:

> *God desires a relationship with you while you are in college. He is in college with you to help guide you towards maximizing your potential and coming into alignment with His purpose for your life.*

God does not want you to operate as if you said your goodbyes to Him, as many did with families and friends at the beginning of the college journey. *God is in college too!* The thing is, however, with all the pressures, temptations and distractions which comes with the journey, you have to be intentional and strategic if you intend to maintain a relationship with God as well as maximize your potential and purpose. He wants to guide you along the journey through the ups, downs, and in-betweens.

As you navigate this book, you will be exposed to practical strategies geared at helping you to:

1. Grow and maintain a relationship with God while in college – even beyond.
2. Cultivate the right mindset and actions for attaining success in college (academically, financially, spiritually and otherwise).
3. Maximize your greatest potential as you come into alignment with the purpose of God for your life.

The strategies in this book are also supported by recounts of real-life college experiences aimed at highlighting the opportunities, pitfalls and snares on the one hand. On the other hand, practical and Biblically sound strategies are also explored in an effort to assist readers in capitalizing on, overcoming or avoiding these issues altogether.

It is my sincere prayer that as you read these books (volumes 1 and 2), the Holy Spirit will minister to you. That He will guide you into effectively using the valuable knowledge and strategies to unearth your greatest potential as you walk in your God-given purpose in college and beyond.

Kayon Rodney

"It's time to break free of the 'little red box' mentality. God is not locked away somewhere waiting on you to let Him out or come to Him."

Kayon Rodney

is

Omnipresent	Omniscient	Omnipotent
• In all places	• All knowing	• All powerful

CHAPTER 1

"LOCK AWAY" with GOD

Man! *College life is a mixture of busy plus busy; the total is busy multiplied by the square root of busy.* Yea. I think you get the gist.

College activities demand so much of your attention that if you are not careful and grounded, you become like a confused kid in a gigantic candy store. Several options but too many selections (distractions) to logically assess the "nutritional" value of the various offerings.

On any given day there are assignment deadlines to meet, group meetings, classes to catch up on, social gatherings, errant and sometimes seemingly inept group members to try and corner, lecturers to assist, lecturers to dodge (*let's be real, that happens too*), responsibilities here, there and everywhere. The name of the game is *decisions, decisions, decisions...*

With all the various tasks competing for your attention, it is easy to get lost in the flurry of activities, and totally ignore spending time with God. The result of this is that you end up walking around with an overburdened mind and an overflowing plate. To avoid this, it is important to make God your "lock away" partner and not a "locked away" partner.

I encourage you to allow God to occupy the most important position in your life. Show Him that this is so by giving Him the best of your time, even when so much else is competing for it. Interestingly, as you do so, you'll begin to realize that other things work out easier and fall into place more. This happens time and again without fail.

GOD AS YOUR "LOCK AWAY" PARTNER

With God as your "*lock away" partner,* you will do things together. You will develop a relationship with Him where you *CHOOSE* to spend time with Him, instead of indulging in some of the other activities competing for your time and attention.

So, you find a nice quiet area or room. In this space and period, you spend time just sitting and talking, writing, listening, singing, worshipping and so on; communing with God, even more than you would with a good friend or a loving parent. Whichever method appeals to you the most during these periods, go right ahead and engage God as such. In these times, you express your thoughts, ideas, feelings and desires, even as you listen to His responses, which the Holy Spirit will bring to the forefront of your thoughts. Responses and principles of course, that will never go contrary to God's Word as contained in the Bible.

The Bible tells us in **Proverbs 3 verses 5-6**, that we should not lean to our own understanding, but in all our ways, acknowledge Him, and He shall direct our paths. Part of following this principle means that you MUST spend time communing with Him about all that is happening with you and asking for His direction in all things.

Technically, being locked away and communing with God in this manner involves variations of praying and worshipping, but not necessarily in the traditional sense or structure, such as being on one's knees. These are relaxed moments between friends, between Father and child. In this safe place you practice communing with God freely, without over-explaining yourself for fear that He will misunderstand your true intent. After all, these barriers don't exist in any communication with God.

He always gets it!

He never misunderstands what you have said or are trying to say. Matter of fact, even when you don't get what you want to say to Him, He still gets it!

Strange, yet most beautiful and comforting.

Another wonderful fact is that we don't have to wonder if we can trust God with our vulnerability. As humans, we tend to "test the waters" as we attempt to identify who we can trust and talk to. Oftentimes, it takes a while before we find persons we want to "open up" to, and if or when we do, there are still some things we will never divulge to them. Our relationship with God transcends all these boundaries. God is confidential, trustworthy, always available to listen, loves you unconditionally and has all the right answers.

Who else can match that?

Absolutely no one else!

LOCK AWAY IN SILENCE: SHHHH! BE QUIET…

How about just sitting with God in silence?

Have you ever tried that?

Just sitting and listening...

No talking or anything, just focusing on God's goodness while listening to hear what He might say to you. I do believe this is one of the hardest things for most Christians to do. Somehow, we always think we need to be talking when we are in the presence of God.

Not so actually...

Learn to be still, and silent before God sometimes.

Try it!

As you do, always take care to assess what you are hearing against the Word of God. If what you are hearing contradicts the Word of God, then nope, that's not of God. Reject that message. Spending time in God's presence in this manner does wonders for training your spiritual ears to discern God's voice when He speaks, among other things!

LOCK AWAY IN SILENCE: WAIT... HE'S QUIET?!

What about the times when God is silent?

Not you being silent now...
God being silent.

Yes, there are those times too. Times when you are seeking God in your lock away times, but hearing nothing.

Nada!

Zilch!

Don't get frustrated.

Silence is part of communication too!

It may be an answer.

An answer to either be still and wait patiently or learn to be comfortable in His presence even when He is silent because He's building your faith to understand that "His silence doesn't mean absence." During these times you learn to rely on His Word, and not become fixated solely on "encounters", or "shimmies and shakes".

Equally, His silence could also be His response to your disobedience and rebellion, like it was with Saul. If you have been walking in rebellion by disobeying His instructions and directions, at some point He will go silent. If this is the case, I would encourage you to genuinely ask His forgiveness and repent (turn) from whatever displeases Him. He is merciful and will forgive.

LOCK AWAY IN HIS PRESENCE...

I encourage you to develop a habit of spending alone time with God – in silence or otherwise. Do not wait until the pressures and challenges are on your shoulders, or are threatening to drown you, before doing so. So, while others are running here and there headfirst into all the "busyness", purpose yourself to lock away with God in this manner, even if just for a few minutes some days.

> **"Lock away"** time **with God** helps with putting things into perspective. It **helps you to gain divine insight into situations and circumstances,** among other things.

This "lock away" time helps you to air and de-clutter your thoughts, put things into perspective and gain divine insight into situations and circumstances. As you cast your burdens on the Lord, you will come to the realization that you are not alone on this journey; He is there as your ever-present Help, Guide, Comforter, Peace, Joy… Need I continue listing all His attributes? You get it!

Oh, another thing…

Just in case you are having a "Laalaa land" view of this lock-away time with God, let's backtrack a little. If you are viewing it as a time where God will rubber-stamp all your actions and grant all your desires like a genie…

Stop right there!

Time to burst that bubble.

POP!!!!

Let me spell out another attribute of God that you might also encounter during your "lock away" times with Him.

The God who chastens those whom He loves…

Sometimes in these "lock away" moments, you will receive some well needed "straightening out". The Bible tells us that whom the Lord loves He chastens, and that we should not despise this chastening (**Hebrews 12:6-11**).

In this "lock away" time, and at other times too, you will get the "chastening" truth. *God's truth*, which will bring conviction and encouragement as to the right course to take regarding matters in which you may need to make amends. He will show you where you went wrong, using His Word as guide. This will no doubt make your flesh feel uncomfortable but will find favour with your Spirit.

After all...

God will never condone wrong no matter how "right" you may feel.

Read that again...

The Bible tells us in **Proverbs 14:12**, that a man's ways seem right in his own eyes, but the end thereof is death. So, though you may feel that you were right or justified about a situation or course of action, as you commune with God in these lock-away moments, you may realize you were totally wrong based on God's principles.

God will never condone wrong no matter how "right" you feel.

Proverbs 14:12 reminds us that our feeling of being "right" might just be a path to death.

Resist the pull of pride and respond quickly and obediently to the corrections you receive in your "lock away" times with God. Do not let sin become a stumbling block to spending time with Him.

Regardless of whether God is speaking in words, silence, or otherwise, be open to embracing the possibilities of this period, as you "lock away" with Him.

GOD AS A "LOCKED AWAY" PARTNER

Oftentimes Christians inadvertently subscribe to the misperception that God is confined to time and locations, such as the church building or the "devotion" spot. Some may also believe God is restricted to wherever the Bible is kept. Of course, these erroneous beliefs translate into actions, as once many are away from these locations they operate as if the omnipresent God is absent and thus unable to see their activities. So, they go off on their own frolics, and in their minds, will only meet up with Him when they return to that area. At that point, they can carry on their religious ritual of "praying", while pretending that God is unaware of some of the "un-Christian like" thoughts and actions they have entertained.

Imagine that!

This brings to mind a song we used to sing as kids;

If I had a little red box,
I'd put my Jesus in.
Then take him out and mwah, mwah, mwah
and put Him right back in!

Mmmmh...

Seriously though, isn't that how many of us treat God? If not all the time, then sometimes – regardless of the justifications that we may attempt to give. Unfortunately, like Judas, many times when we "take" Jesus out of the "little red box", it is to kiss Him (pray, worship, praise) with a betrayer's lips.

How so?

Well, by then we would have ignored His leading in our daily thoughts and affairs, and fallen into all manner of sin (idolatry, disobedience, fornication, lying, cheating, stealing, gossiping, slander, murder, and so on).

> **<u>Lip check-up:</u>**
>
> What kind of lips have you been "kissing" Jesus with?
>
> **Are they the lips of a betrayer or a friend?**

"Whoa now!"

"Murder?"

"Isn't that a far jump?", you might have thought after reading the previous "sin-list".

Well…

Allow me to digress a little.

In case "murder" jumped out at you as being, "*<u>a sin most extreme</u>*", and not to be included among those mentioned afore, then here's a quick clarification. ***Many Christians are guilty of murder, and even worse, are repeat offenders who approach God daily as unremorseful, unrepentant murderers.***

You see, murder, as explained in the Bible, differs slightly from the world's explanation. Where the world says murder is to cause death by intentionally inflicting harm to someone, the Bible says in **1 John 3:15,** that "*Whosoever hateth his brother is a murderer....*" In other words, if you have been harbouring hate against others in your heart, then, according to God's word, you are a murderer. Spiritually, that means you are in league with the vilest convicted murderer! You just haven't physically acted on that hate to match the world's definition of murder... at least not yet.

That's a hard pill to swallow, isn't it?

Hard, but it is the truth.

A kick to the flesh but a boost to the Spirit...

Once again I ask, what kind of lips have you been kissing God with?

Also, is your hand stained with your brother's blood?

These questions should cause you to pause and do a spiritual check of your lips and hands before going before God, especially for your "lock away" times with Him. If the spiritual check reveals that you are a "Judas", don't despair however, this is an opportunity to make it right. Ask God's forgiveness and repent of the sin. Let Him teach you how to love (and forgive where necessary), especially those whom you find hardest to love. It is possible by God's grace. Don't lock God out by putting Him into the "little red box"; treating

Him like a "locked away" partner. Choose to give Him unrestrained access to every part of your life.

The truth is, you cannot divorce your daily thoughts and actions from your "spiritual life" and then consider yourself a faithful Christian in a fulfilling relationship with God. It is your spiritual principles that should guide your daily activities, and this cannot be done effectively if you operate from a mindset of locking God away in a static location or time – the proverbial "little red box".

Therefore, don't make the mistake of thinking you can lock God into the "little red box" mentality and retrieve Him at will. For example, when you desperately need that passing grade or need a miracle so the tuition can be paid in time for you to sit the exams. It just doesn't work that way. That's an opportunistic mindset, not a relational one. I encourage you to change that mindset if this applies to you.

THERE ARE DAYS I LIKE TO BE...

College teaches you a lot that will impact your actions and attitude for the rest of your life. You get to determine whether these lessons will impact you for good or bad. Take for example myself and learning to be alone with God. A lot of the knowledge I am now sharing, came out of a rough process.

There were times I would be so caught up with assignments and all manner of other things that I neglected to spend enough alone time with God. Always and without fail, whenever this happened, I would become painfully aware, as there would always be a ripple effect in other areas of my life. Everything would start getting more confusing and tumultuous; basically, just falling apart. I would snap at my daughter and husband, feel overburdened, pressured, irritable, and became easily angered. I began to discern a pattern and came to the realization that the less time I spent locked away with God, the more the cares of this world and college life would hammer me into the ground.

I remember one night it got so *bad* that I felt as if I just could not make it. This was it! I really needed to talk to God!

What did I do?

I obeyed the yearning in my Spirit, went to a quiet place and offloaded my burdens. I sat down and just talked to God as if He were sitting right there beside me. At that moment I was not focusing on my numerous assignments that needed to be completed; my daughter or her numerous assignments that also needed to be done; my husband who was probably in one of his withdrawn and terse moods because I had been neglecting him; nor the business and everything else that needed my attention. My focus was on meeting with God; telling Him how I was feeling. It was not about trying to find the "right words", being "scripturally correct", or "sounding right". I just needed to talk to my Father and friend. Plain and simple...

And talked I did!

As I began to lay all my burdens on Him, I could literally feel the difference. The burden kept getting lighter and lighter. I stayed in that place for a while, just talking about it all and letting Him know what was happening, and how I felt. I explained that I was falling apart at the seams and needed His help.

There is just something amazing that happens when you are talking with God that just doesn't happen with anyone else. *You experience a sense of connection that is unmatched...* A feeling that you do not have to dot all the i's and cross all the t's, or provide the deep background that you would need to share with someone else, in an attempt to make them understand what you are experiencing. Somehow there is an unspoken understanding and reassurance that God knows exactly what the situation is, and so you can focus more on just talking freely and listening.

Something amazing happens when you are talking with God, that just doesn't happen with anyone else!

You do not have to dot all the i's and cross all the t's! God knows exactly what the situation is, even more than you do quite frankly.

So, I talked, He listened. His presence reassured.

By the end of this conversation with my “lock away” partner, I felt so light. I couldn’t help smiling. Not because the troubles had disappeared, but because I somehow felt better from having cast all my cares on God. I no longer felt as if I was in this alone and that was reassuring. I just knew He would take care of everything.

As the lightness surrounded me, my Spirit started singing:

There are days I like to be

all alone with Christ my Lord

I can tell Him of my troubles all alone...

I found this so calming, yet quite strange. Strange because I knew that was a very old hymn and wondered where it came from. Just that portion.

Was there more to it?

What was God trying to say to me?

Of course, I was curious about the lyrics of the song, so I hit up the “go-to” source for college students. This one source which wears many hats in one...

GOOGLE.

Yup! Google.

I didn’t know the lyrics of the hymn except for the portion that kept replaying in my Spirit, and I wanted to know more. As I researched, what came up were the full lyrics of a church hymn; “All Alone” by G.T. Byrd. I poured over the lines and found that it expressed exactly the situation that I had just experienced.

It spoke of how:

On Mount Olive's sacred brow
Jesus spent the night in pray'r,
He's the pattern for us all, all alone.
If we'll only steal away
in some portion of the day,
we will find it always pays to be alone.

Refrain

There are times I'd like to be
All alone with Christ my Lord,
I can tell Him of my troubles all alone.

The hymn goes on to speak of how when we are alone with Christ, we can tell Him of our sorrows and grief and find quick relief. It speaks of God always imparting grace to a weary saddened heart, at the end of which we receive joy sublime (uplifting joy and peace).

It is just amazing how effective the Holy Spirit is at bringing things to our attention or remembrance when we need it the most. If only we would learn to quiet our hearts more often so we can discern His move.

Just Wow!

I truly experienced everything that the hymn spoke of! I felt comforted in my Spirit from having spent that much-needed time alone locked away in the presence of God.

Who knew the joy that an old hymn could bring to a young soul in such a time of need? Especially one coming from a background of hating the very sight of the hymn book being pulled out in church as a kid; as that would mean some drawn-out, drab singing of "boring, old hymns". In honesty, that's how they sounded to me at the time.

How ironic it is that God would provide rest for my weary, beaten soul using what I once despised...

For the record, I no longer despise hymns or see them as drab or boring - thank God! Matter of fact, with some of the music masquerading as "gospel" and "praise and worship" songs these days, the beauty and timeless value of these old "songs of praise and adoration", hold even greater significance to me.

What's the main take-away from all this?

There will always be several things competing for your time and attention in college, as matter of fact not just in college, but the world in general. In spite of all this, choose to spend time with God as your lock away partner. Don't treat Him like a "locked away" partner. Spending alone time with God is a must! Not just when you feel weary and burdened either, but also when you are happy and excited.

Practise making God your "lock away" partner until it becomes one of your favourite pastimes. In those times, God will provide divine guidance, instruction, and correction as necessary. So, just get away from the crowd and spend some time of the day in God's presence. This is for your own good, growth, sanity and wellbeing!

LET'S REFLECT!

Having read this chapter, what are some important points that you'd like to note?

Note to self...

*"**Apart from God, you are your greatest asset on this journey - not so much the paper at the end!** Take care of your spiritual, mental and emotional well-being."*

Kayon Rodney

I give up
suicide
overwhelmed
incapable
assignments
failure
sadness
depression
failure
pressure
tired
I CAN'T DO THIS!
suicide
tired
pressure
not good enough
frustration
Rest
Fun
God
Relax
Rest
Pray
Fun
Relax
Relax
God
Self Care
Pray
God
Rest
wisdom
Fun
Rest
faith

CHAPTER 2

SELF MANAGEMENT & CARE

No one ever goes to college with the goal of having mental breakdowns or at the extreme tip of the scale, committing suicide – becoming a statistic.

I apologize for not easing you into this section…

However, if this jolts you to the seriousness of the matter and stays at the back of your mind, propelling you to seek help when needed, then my job would've been complete.

The fact is that mental breakdowns and suicide among college students are two of the more extreme results stemming from the inability of many students to handle stress in a healthy manner. While these two are "the more extreme", they are interestingly, not as rare as one might think. Matter of fact, in the U.S., suicide was listed as the "*#2 leading cause of death for college students*" as revealed by a 2016 study conducted by Roseik and colleagues. Bear in mind, of course, that this does not include the statistics for the many who would have "*attempted*" suicide within the period. The statistics for "*attempted suicides*" vary but also indicate a troubling situation.

Another research conducted by Schwartz in 2016, for example, found that in the US alone, over 2 million college students admitted to having seriously considered committing suicide, while 300,000 actually made an attempt to carry out the act.

Alarming!!

Not to be overlooked either is the role that depression plays in fueling many of these suicidal thoughts. Depression and anxiety are real threats to the mental health of college students, and are often two of the key players in suicides and attempted suicides. In a 2021 article by the Mayo Clinic Health System, titled, "*What parents need to know about college students and depression*", it was highlighted that symptoms of anxiety and depression were recorded in up to 44% of college students. You see, the issue is quite real and also quite prevalent; many college students suffer from anxiety and depression. *Quite troubling...*

I have gone through the pains of highlighting these statistics not to scare anyone into fearing the college environment; but more so, that you can be prepared to address potentially stressful situations before they get to extreme levels, such as anxiety attacks, depression and suicide.

Of course, you may wonder...

But what's driving all this?

Well, the short answer to that is that there may be a combination of reasons which may cause students to feel stressed to the point of depression, mental breakdowns and even suicide. For example, several students find themselves incapable of handling the physical (and to some extent, emotional) transition from home to college. For many, it is the first time they are away from their homes and family. This, coupled with navigating an arduous high stakes environment, heightened demands for academic performance, and heavy class schedules, naturally, can make life particularly challenging.

In addition, many experience culture shock, made woefully worse by their lack of sufficient life skills. Of course, the ever-present social and financial challenges also make the list. Then to top it all off, these issues might also be further exacerbated by experimenting with drugs and alcohol which can further lessen one's ability to think rationally and make sound decisions.

Not to be overlooked either, are the sometimes unexpected painful and traumatic experiences faced by some students while in college. These often range in type and intensity but have devastating effects and take a toll on the mental state of many students.

I mean... How can they not?

Imagine having to deal with an assault, rape, separation, divorce, or the death of a family member on top of everything else that comes with the college experience! Those are not scenarios that we even want to imagine, let alone experience. However, this has been and is the sad reality for some college students. *Hurting but pursuing...*

So, you see, there is no shortage of stressors and potentially stressful situations while in college.

And that's the short answer...

STOP, TAKE STOCK, CHANGE COURSE

With the above background information under your belt, it is now time to proactively address the issue of *"college stress"*, with a view to helping you identify and effectively manage stressful periods in college. The starting point is with you.

It starts with knowing you...

Knowing how you react under pressure and potentially negative situations provide a good benchmark for being able to identify when to *stop, take stock and change course.*

Let's break this down some more.

How do you react to feeling pressured, overwhelmed, and so on?

Do you:

- *pray?*
- *talk to family or friends?*
- *snap at others?*
- *suffer from anxiety and panic attacks?*
- *shut down and become emotionally distant?*
- *isolate yourself?*
- *resort to crying?*
- *turn to alcohol, sex or drugs?*
- *find an artistic outlet to express yourself?*
- *attempt to logically sort through emotions and issues?*
- *adopt the attitude that "the sky is falling"?*
- *stifle your emotions and put your focus elsewhere?*

How about some of the triggers that might cause you to react in the manner you have identified (whether from the list above or self-supplied)?

Is it:

- *fear of failure?*
- *lack of sleep?*
- *feeling as if things are out of control?*
- *frustration?*

- *worry?*
- *disappointment?*
- *betrayal?*
- *rejection?*
- *overthinking?*

These questions are meant to help get you started on identifying and appropriately managing stressors and potential triggers.

Just to be clear...

It is quite normal for everyone to experience some amount of stress daily. Matter of fact, stress is not necessarily a bad thing. It is how we handle stress that determines whether the outcome is good or bad. For example, stress can actually be channelled into increased focus, innovativeness, creativity and greater productivity as you double down to meet the demands of the pressure being exerted by a situation.

Stress is not necessarily **a bad thing.**

It is how we **handle the stress** that determines whether **the outcome is good** or bad

However, if you find yourself being held hostage to stress and digging emotional and psychological graves with your thoughts and reactions, then this is where you need to change course and address the matter in a healthy way.

TIPS FOR COPING WITH HIGH-STRESS PERIODS

Here are some of the tips and strategies that many, including myself, have used. You may also find these useful for overcoming stressful periods in college:

1 GOD at the centre of it all.

Maintain open and constant communication with God. Do not leave God out of the college experience whether good, bad, or indifferent. Develop a relationship with Him where you commune with Him about every and anything. Whether you are up at 3 am completing an assignment and possibly on the verge of tears because of how overwhelming it all seems, or just checked your grades and found yourself with an 'A' for an exam or course.

Pray, read and apply the Word of God. Find hope, solace and inspiration for your times of need in His Word. Allow Him to be your Rock. The one you run to without having to wonder if you are being a bother, or if He is able to help.

Talk to Him!

Be open about your fears, challenges, expectations and needs. After all, His Word reminds you in **1 Peter 5:7,** that you should "*Give all your worries and cares to God, for he cares about you*" (NLT version). That right there is priceless comfort and reassurance. Especially in light of the fact that He not only cares for you but reaffirms His promise to "*... keep him in perfect peace, whose mind is stayed on thee: because he trusteth in thee*" – **Isaiah 26:3.** Therefore, when you live a lifestyle of laying all your cares on God and keep your mind trusting in His promises, faithfulness, and so on, He will, in turn, keep you in "perfect peace".

Perfect peace...

This doesn't mean the absence of storms or pressures, but rather, choosing to focus on and trust God in the middle of them.

Personally, God was and is my greatest source of help, hope and peace for all things (stressful, confusing and otherwise) while in college and even now. **HE HAS NEVER FAILED ME!** He will not fail you either. Imagine having access to a God who delights in taking your burdens and stressors, even while teaching you to cope or overcome them.

Man!!

That's a thought I can't even fully begin to grasp, and I am left in awe and as aptly expressed by the psalmist in ***Psalm 139:6****...*

"Such knowledge is too wonderful for me; it is high, I cannot attain unto it."

But...

I am grateful, and I'm sure you are too.

2

Exercise discernment

Ask God to increase your discernment and wisdom so you can accurately assess people and situations so as to make the right decisions. Discernment revolves around the keen ability to grasp and understand finer and often obscure (and unvoiced) details and intent behind words, actions, and situations.

How does discernment look?

There is no one answer to that question really. There is no literal dinging bell that goes off when discernment kicks in, nor a literal radiance from a bulb being turned on.

Aaahhmm... that's way out.

Like cartoon-level way out!

While there is no set or static method signifying "discernment", however, here are a few examples of discernment in action:

The Holy Spirit impresses a "gut feeling", a "sixth sense" type of vibe about a particular situation, person or choice. It is this innate feeling that something is right, or conversely, that something just isn't right or adding up and you should exercise caution in your decisions.

The Holy Spirit is also able to warn you to pull back when you are approaching danger zones, especially in your thoughts and actions. For example, you find yourself folding under confusion and pressure, almost to the point of anxiety, then seemingly out of nowhere the thought comes that "*God is not the author of confusion*", and *"be anxious about nothing"*.

The Holy Spirit may also impress upon you that you need to take a break, step back, put down that assignment for a few minutes and so on. That's the power of having the ever-present Spirit of Truth, Comfort and Guidance – the Holy Spirit, regulating your thoughts and actions as you exercise discernment

Find and utilize "de-pressurizing" or "de-stressing" routines and "safe zones"

An important practice to develop is that of finding a "safe zone" of sorts which you utilize for the purpose of taking a break when things begin to feel overwhelming. Use this safe zone to step back from everything as you take a break. It may be a nice, quiet spot on or off-campus (indoor or outdoor) where you can shut out everything and just indulge in an activity which helps to take your mind off the other seemingly overwhelming situations. During these times you may pray, read, listen to some uplifting music, draw, write or journal, watch a few funny videos, and so on.

While the enemy would want you to remain in a negative place and be overwhelmed to the point of anxiety or a nervous breakdown, the Holy Spirit directs you to step back a little, release the tension and then try again. Identify a safe zone early on in your studies. Somewhere that makes you feel at ease. Somewhere you can go just to take a break.

Please note, however...

> *The Holy Spirit will not push you to shirk your responsibilities under the guise of taking seemingly unending breaks.*

Nope...

> *Sounds more like the spirit of procrastination in that regard.*

For me, I had two main "safe zones" that I would often retreat to when I needed to take and break and "de-stress or de-pressurize". One was the guestroom at my home and the other was in my car parked somewhere on campus. In addition, I would also take breaks and indulge in some of my favourite pastimes, such as watching HGTV, Discovery Channel or any other activity I consider to be fun.

In these safe zones and breaks, you refuse to give in to negative feelings or focus on the several issues that threaten to overwhelm your sanity. Instead choose to release them, even for that moment in time, as you focus on the other activities.

4 **Maintain contact with support systems**

While college can sometimes feel like a flurry of never-ending activities, one thing you must make time for is keeping in touch with support systems. Support systems are important on this journey.

Do not neglect to maintain contact with and visit family, friends, church and other support systems as much as you are able to. How calming and comforting it can be when you receive a much-needed call filled with laughter and updates on the happenings back home or at church!

Times like these help to pull your attention from being so totally "college absorbed". Reminding you that:

"*There is still life happening outside of college*" and

"*This period is only for now, not the rest of your life*".

These support systems also remind you that many people are rooting for you, praying for you, and loving you, even if they are not within your immediate environment.

In addition, if you feel the need to, schedule regular sessions with your college's guidance counsellor. This is especially beneficial for students who do not have supportive family systems or those who may be undergoing issues which require additional help from a trained professional. Do not be afraid to utilize these avenues of help. There is usually at least one available on each campus.

How about support in the form of your pastor and church family? Or, from Christian groups on campus? Yes, these also form part of the support system that students have access to as they traverse the college experience.

Personally, I have seen several students receive much-needed help from all the avenues discussed above. They provide invaluable assistance in helping students to work through issues and challenges so that they do not fall off the wagon and into mental breakdowns, or worse. Many students have been saved from the brink of nervous breakdowns, even suicide, because of intervention. Do not allow pride to prevent you from seeking help from these support systems if you need to do so.

5 **Take a break and regroup if necessary**

Admitting you need help or that you need to take a break is not an admission of failure. Far from it actually! It is a show of wisdom when it is warranted, and exercising wisdom is never failure. Sometimes a break is just what is needed. For various reasons, many students have found it necessary to put their studies on pause so they can regroup emotionally, physically, mentally and financially.

> **Admitting that you need help** or that you need to take a break **is not an admission of failure.**
>
> It is a show of wisdom when warranted.

Oftentimes, the challenges are so overwhelming that some students are just incapable of effectively maneuvering them at present. So instead of allowing the situation to totally spiral out of control, some make the wise decision to request some time off from their studies (leave of absence). This may range from a few days or weeks off, or alternately, deferring their studies for a more extended period such as a semester, and so on. Of course, this is not a light matter, nor one to be opted for unadvisedly based on knee-jerk reactions to a "*little*" stress. Hence the importance of consulting with a responsible voice of reason such as parents or one of the professionals prior to making such decisions – especially when considering deferring one's studies for extended periods.

Many students have made the wise decision of taking a break from their studies when they found it to be ABSOLUTELY necessary. Most of these students have also gone on to successfully complete their studies after returning from their break. Oftentimes the break greatly assists with helping to put things into perspective, making the requisite plans for going forward, as well as providing a period for mental rejuvenation, among other things.

Take careful note...

Taking a break, however, while having the benefit of allowing students to regroup and return, also has the potential pitfall of students not returning to complete their studies. Hence my advice is not to choose this option unadvisedly (on a whim) without discussing same with a responsible voice of reason and without having a return plan in mind.

The bottom line is that the college journey is rarely ever straightforward. With every twist and turn, however, we can use our God-given wisdom to successfully navigate the experience.

Here's the bottom line...

The inescapable fact...

The college period is more often than not, a high-stress one. For most students, this comes with assignment deadlines to meet, a spiritual and social life to nurture, all while attempting to balance and manage scarce resources, new ideas, old and new friends, family, lecturers, courses, exams... you name it!

Yet...

Many, like myself, have successfully maneuvered.

It is also possible for you.

While experiencing some amount of stress can actually be beneficial, the inability to effectively handle stress has been the downfall of many students. This has often resulted in several adverse effects, such as anxiety, depression, mental breakdowns and even suicidal thoughts and attempts for some students. Unfortunately, some have also successfully carried out the act of committing suicide.

This does not have to be the case, however.

You can learn to manage stress in a healthy manner, utilizing it as a motivating rather than destructive force. As you traverse the college journey be watchful for the signs and symptoms of stress overload. Don't just stop at identifying the symptoms, but deal with the issues decisively once they've been identified. Pull on all avenues of help and support to help you overcome high-stress periods- which, quite frankly, are inevitable and come with the territory. Exercise self-care and manage the period, including any and all associated areas of stress by relying first and foremost on God's help and guidance. In addition, utilize "safe zones" and various support systems as may be necessary.

Keep this thought tucked at the back of your mind always:

> ***Apart from God, you are your greatest asset on this journey.*** *Your spiritual, mental and emotional well-being… not so much the paper at the end of the journey.*
>
> After all…
>
> *A degree at the expense of your mental, physical and emotional health, or even life, is of no value to you or anyone.*

LET'S REFLECT!

Having read this chapter, what are some important points that you'd like to note?

Note to self...

Time for "book smart" to meet "street smart". Arrange the meeting or suffer the consequences.

Kayon Rodney

Experiential Learning
Wisdom & Discernment
Street Smart
Emotional Intelligence
Situational Intelligence

CHAPTER 3

STREET SMART

Aim for being both "book smart" and "street smart".

Why is "street smart" in a book about the "college experience"?

Well, you see...

Street smart is not just for the "streets", it is also crucial for navigating the college experience, indeed life. While being book smart is concerned with knowledge gained primarily through books and academics, street smart relies on using practical experience and situational understanding to make the right judgement and take the appropriate actions when needed. In college, matter of fact, in life, street smart is often seen as trumping book smart.

Unfortunately, many students are book smart but not street smart.

Many are excelling academically but failing at reading the cues and being alert to the intents of others and the many happenings in their surroundings. That is, until it is oftentimes too late.

This is not ok. Definitely not ok.

In college, you need to have your "wits" (discernment, wisdom, and intuition) about you. After you have prayed, you still need to be, as the Bible puts it in **Matthew 10:16**, *"...wise as serpents, harmless as doves."*

STREET SMART IN ACTION

One, being street smart pulls on your ability to accurately read people and situations and respond appropriately relying on discernment, wisdom and emotional intelligence. Without the right mix, match and application of this trio, you have no chance of being "street smart".

Two, being street smart goes a far way in helping you to navigate what could otherwise be uncomfortable, compromising, dangerous and even potentially deadly situations. This of course, requires an acute awareness of self, others and situations. It also involves understanding potential triggers for danger zones in yourself, others and situations as well as how to navigate these successfully.

An acute awareness of self, in this regard, includes being aware of how you respond when you are overwhelmed. This is crucial to averting danger zones such as impulsive and unwise decisions and coping strategies; or falling victim to anxiety, depression, self-harming and even suicidal thoughts to name a few.

Equally, being aware of the propensity of potentially compromising situations (such as excessive drinking at a party) in leading to the loss of inhibitions and self-control, surely provides a guideline for making wiser decisions. While self-help books and experts may try to explain and walk you through these scenarios, it is your ability to discern and manage the situations as they unfold, your "street smarts", that will ultimately make the difference.

The truth is...

The essence of being street smart is not limited to particular topics or static scenarios, nor can it be wholly taught. It requires employing good judgement and wisdom and responsibility in differing situations. No book or course can ever teach you all there is to learn about being street smart. It is a daily and experiential-based process. With that being made clear, there is however certain basic knowledge which can help to prepare your minds as you seek to be street smart on your college journey.

> **Street smart** is a daily and experiential-based process of **employing good judgement, wisdom and responsibility in differing situations**.
>
> No book or course can ever teach you all there is to learn about being street smart.

This is where this book comes in...

It is your ability to process and apply the background information along with experiential knowledge to varying decisions, that will count as wisdom or lack thereof. One of the first steps I will take you through is what I like to call, "de-ostracizing".

Yes "de-ostracizing"...

That's not a typo.

Rather, it is an invitation to remove your head from the sand and face the facts, some of which will be outlined throughout this chapter. Knowledge is key. Application of that knowledge to reality opens the door for wisdom and street smart to step in.

Try to keep up!

WHAT THE NUMBERS ARE SAYING...

While many students start college with a long mental checklist of things to do and try while in college, there is often little thought given to maintaining their safety while pursuing these experiences. Yet, a simple search online would reveal frightening results on the prevalence of college campus crimes and crimes against college students. These crimes range from robbery, theft, burglary, sexual assaults (fondling, rape and so on), abductions, aggravated assault, and to a lesser extent, murder.

An April 2022 article titled "Campus Safety Guide" by Marisa Upson, revealed that in the United States for the year 2019, there were "*...nearly 28,000 on-campus crimes, burglaries accounted for over 9,000 and forcible sex offenses accounted for almost 12,000.*" While the numbers may not seem overly alarming based on overall college enrolment, when those numbers are matched to real victims (human beings like you and myself), then it hits differently. Added to that is the background that those are just the "reported" statistics for the US, which do not take into consideration those that go unreported.

Take for example incidences of rape and attempted rapes; in a 2000 study conducted by Fisher, Cullen and Turner, it was revealed that less than "*5% of completed and attempted rapes were reported to law enforcement officials.*"

Let that sink in...

That means, if we were to do a projection based on the 12,000 reported in 2019 and assume that those were "the less than 5%", then the magnitude of the situation would balloon beyond what one would even care to imagine.

College crimes are quite prevalent. These include robbery, theft, burglary, sexual assaults, abductions and aggravated assault.

BE ON GUARD!

You do the math!

How about in other countries around the world... Say the Caribbean, for example?

While statistics are not always as readily available for the Caribbean as for the U.S. and a few other countries, the stories abound of various crimes committed against students on and off college campuses. You see... this issue of student safety is in no way limited to first or third-world countries. It is a world and college-wide challenge.

Of course, it is worth mentioning here as well, that the perpetrators are not always strangers, but most often than not, are other students and even faculty members. Therefore, be on guard.

Be wise as serpents, harmless as doves...

THE COMMON FACTORS OF THE PROBLEM

While victims and perpetrators differ in each circumstance, there are certain characteristics that can be tracked as being common to most college crimes. Some of these include:

- the prevalence of unabated drinking and often associated experimental and social drug use which are common to the college culture;
- obsessions;
- spurned love interests;
- jealousy;
- negative sociocultural background of perpetrators;

- possible unaddressed mental illnesses; and
- victims' false sense of security.

Of course, the list above is by no means exhaustive. It is, however, reflective of the atmosphere that prevails on most, if not all, college campuses.

Even as there are several contributing factors in the perpetuation of college crimes, there are also a myriad of negative effects that stem from these attacks against life and property. Crimes on campus often rob students (both victims and the rest of the campus population) of their sense of safety, independence and freedom. In their wake, victims and other students are often left traumatized, fearful, and distracted. Of course, one can imagine that these have correlated effects. For example, the poor academic performance of some students, and their general unwillingness to be actively engaged in the college social scene in the aftermath of these crimes.

Crimes on campus often rob the campus population of its sense of safety, independence and freedom.

This may also lead to other issues such as poor academic performance, depression, self-harm, suicide, and so on…

If not appropriately handled then these feelings could also progress to issues of depression, poor academic performance, self-harm, suicide, and even victims becoming perpetrators themselves. The ripple effects are far-reaching.

There is a saying that goes, *"to be forewarned is to be forearmed"*. This is the objective of this chapter. To provide you with sufficient information to assist you in making wise (street smart) decisions instead of acting foolishly due to naivete. It is to provide background information which will help to support your ability to be street smart in college, and even beyond.

STREET SMARTS – KEEPING SAFE

So, here's the deal...

As highlighted earlier in the chapter, it is impossible to provide you with specific "street smart" information to address all the potential situations you may face. However, there are a few invaluable nuggets of wisdom which I can share with you for use as you navigate the college journey. The list below is but a drop in the bucket and you might find yourself thinking of others as you go along!

And that's great!

That means you would have started conditioning your mind to be "street smart"!

1 TRUST YOUR "*GUT*" INSTINCTS...

Have you ever heard or repeated these words?

Somehow I just knew something wasn't right!

I could feel it in my guts!

Many times, what people refer to as a "gut feeling" is the Holy Spirit's way of directing our attention to something that doesn't look or feel right. It's a feeling of unease that we just can't always seem to explain.

So, some people say, "trust your guts"! In Christendom we often say, trust the Holy Spirit's leading.

And you know what?

That "gut feeling" is oftentimes never wrong either.

Therefore, if you feel unsettled or uncomfortable about a person, course of action, situation or so, slow down and assess some more before making a decision you might regret. Carefully examine the reasons why you might be feeling the way you are.

Don't just brush your gut feelings aside.

Part of assessing, of course, includes prayer (asking for discernment and revelation), further observation, avoiding impulsive decisions, and even seeking advice from a reputable and responsible source.

Please note I said "reputable and responsible" ...

Don't give your ears to any and everyone. The implications of doing so might cost you dearly.

Remember...

Examine these "gut feelings", and don't ignore them!

2 LEARN YOUR WAY AROUND CAMPUS

Aside from the orientation tour, learn your way around the campus. Consider exploring the campus during periods of high traffic when there are many people around, and you do not have a class. Don't just isolate yourself to your dorm or areas within your immediate vision. Knowing your campus is of utmost importance as this will provide you with:

- a mental map of the various areas and how to plan the most effective, efficient and safest routes to and from classes and so on (whether by day or night);
- an idea of alternate routes that you can use in case of emergencies;
- how to access assistance if needed. For example - the various security posts, or on-campus police (if any).

If available, be sure to download a campus map to assist you in learning the physical layout and even sociocultural microcosms of your campus. The above reasons represent few of the many important reasons why you should know your campus.

3 SECURE YOUR PERSON

✓ Avoid walking alone after dark – walk in groups, or at least with one other person. For students on larger campuses, there might be campus escort shuttle. Utilize this service if available.

- ✓ Carry small LEGAL protective items – these may include, whistles, alarms and pepper spray. Please be sure to research what is legal to carry based on the laws of the country where your campus is. For example, in some Caribbean countries, it is illegal for civilians to own and carry pepper spray. Therefore, do your due diligence.
- ✓ Say no to drugs, smoking and alcohol – alcohol and drugs impair one's ability to make wise decisions and therefore the user becomes more susceptible to becoming a victim of some college crimes, such as sexual assaults, robbery and kidnapping.

In addition to alcohol and drugs, smoking (including vaping), though known to be bad for your health, is also another temptation in college. Smoking and vaping are often used as potential avenues for easing stress and pressures. However, do not make unwise decisions by opening Pandora's box as a potential fix for a temporary situation. Find healthy and safe coping mechanisms for whatever issues you might face.

Unhealthy coping mechanisms get more creative and addictive by the day too…

For example, one can gain access to mood-altering and hallucinogenic drugs sold in the form of candies, brownies and so on (if you know where to look). Then there are the prescription and black-market drugs that some students abuse. Some of these include drugs for staying awake, relaxing, increased energy and the list goes on. Though quite dangerous, there is no shortage or lack of access to these drugs in college.

Unfortunately, whether out of curiosity, peer pressure or trying to find a quick fix for handling the stress and pressures of college, many students get sucked into using mood and perception-altering drugs. Some of these include dangerous, yet popular drugs such as marijuana, magic mushrooms, bath salts, methylenedioxy-methamphetamine (MDMA) (more popularly known on the streets as Molly, Adam, Hug, Love Drug, Scooby snacks, Beans, E, Clarity, Roll, Snowball, X, Ecstasy, or XTC). Drugs are usually taken in capsules, tablets, powder or liquid form, and in the case of marijuana, smoked. These drugs give users a "high" in the moment by affecting the brain's function resulting in altered moods, thoughts and behaviours.

Of course, persons often give little or no thought to the risks associated with using these and other drugs. Some adverse effects of using these drugs include impaired judgement, faintness, chills, a drastic increase in heart rate and blood pressure, depression, issues with memory and information retention, and of course, addiction. The danger of taking these and other drugs becomes even more frightening when one considers that many times they might be laced with other dangerous drugs, chemicals and ingredients.

There is not enough space in this book to outline all the drugs and their dangers. There is simply too much to cover. However, you can embark on your own research online for greater depth regarding drug abuse in college.

Here is the bottom line however...

Regardless of the temptations in college, drugs or otherwise...

Know what you are about!

Don't yield to curiosity, pressures and temptations.

It's not worth it!

✓ <u>Exercise care when gathering socially</u> – Be alert at social gatherings. For example **secure your edible items** to prevent tampering from unscrupulous persons. Especially for females, the stories abound of victims who were drugged and sexually assaulted, stemming from their incapacitation due to "date rape drugs" being put into their drinks or food. Of course, unattended food items provide easy targets for perpetrators. In addition, be careful about accepting offers of drink and food from persons you have just met or barely know. Even more, **never accept food or drink from persons you don't trust, or food or drink that seems suspicious**- even if it's from someone you know.

Of course, there are several other aspects of vigilance which you should employ as you gather socially. These are merely a few to get your thoughts rolling in the right direction. Practice being both wise and vigilant when gathering socially.

SECURE YOUR POSSESSIONS

Get this in your head quickly...

Living on campus or in a shared apartment is not the same as living at home with your family. There are more moving parts, and bodies than you can always safely account for, coming and going.

Leaving your things lying around unsecured is not advised!

Don't let your belongings become an easy target for burglars and thieves. Therefore, as much as possible, *"Lock up and Lockdown"*. Lock away important items. Lock your car doors and dorm rooms whenever you will be away from them.

In some instances, securing your possessions in your apartment or dorm might require you to provide your own lock and key storage, such as lockboxes. These lockboxes come in all sizes, shapes and forms to suit the needs of students and can even be purchased online. Or if you cannot afford one, how about running a quick DIY project and making one? You could also secure the help of a cabinet maker to help you in this process, if necessary.

Owning or having access to a lockbox should work well enough for securing your most important items; especially considering that electronics, cash, credit and debit cards, electronic devices, textbooks, and jewelry are some of the most often targeted items for those with "*sticky fingers*". These are mostly small items and should fit easily enough into your lockbox and provide some amount of security.

5 WATCH YOUR SOCIAL MEDIA USAGE & SETTINGS

There is a tendency these days for most persons to place their every move and anticipated actions on social media for the world to see. While this may seem fun and harmless, it can certainly be dangerous. It provides easy tracking for perpetrators to keep tabs on you and make plans which could result in you being harmed.

Equally, be sure to turn off "location" services on your social media accounts to prevent easy tracking by persons you do not wish to keep tabs on your whereabouts.

6 EMERGENCY CONTACTS

Keep emergency contacts close at hand (for example, saved in your phone, or printed and kept in a visible area of your dorm room or apartment). These emergency contacts should include your emergency contact persons, campus security, police and other pertinent persons and services. Having your emergency contacts information easily accessible becomes especially important in emergencies, when one might have challenges finding the numbers needed.

Be sure to memorize a few of these numbers as well. After all... what if you lose your phone or do not have access to it and have to make urgent contact with someone? Yea... the "*dinosaur method*" of mentally storing some emergency numbers can become a lifesaver.

Another important strategy is that of configuring the Emergency/SOS feature that is available on most cellphones or can be downloaded as an app. These apps allow users to add one or more emergency contacts; persons who will be contacted in an emergency by the push of a button the requisite number of times from your cellphone. This is especially helpful if you are in a situation where speed and being covert are important. The benefit of this is that emergency contacts can be called without even unlocking your phone or searching for a number. There are even additional features of some of these apps, whereby once activated, there is automatic tracking and video footage of the users and their surroundings.

Talk about using technology to aid in your safety and security, and this certainly makes the list!

<u>The fact of the matter is</u>... it makes sense to be wise as serpents and harmless as doves as you navigate the college experience. Street smart can sustain you where book smart

can only dream of treading. Therefore... you need both as you traverse the college journey.

While not exhaustive, the prior information and tips on being street smart and maintaining your safety and security in college is sure to get your attention. Aim to take the necessary steps to navigate the college experience using both street and book smarts. Exercise discernment and wisdom in all your choices. This could be the difference between becoming a part of the crime statistics which prevail on many campuses, or safely completing your studies.

LET'S REFLECT!

Having read this chapter, what are some important points that you'd like to note?

Note to self...

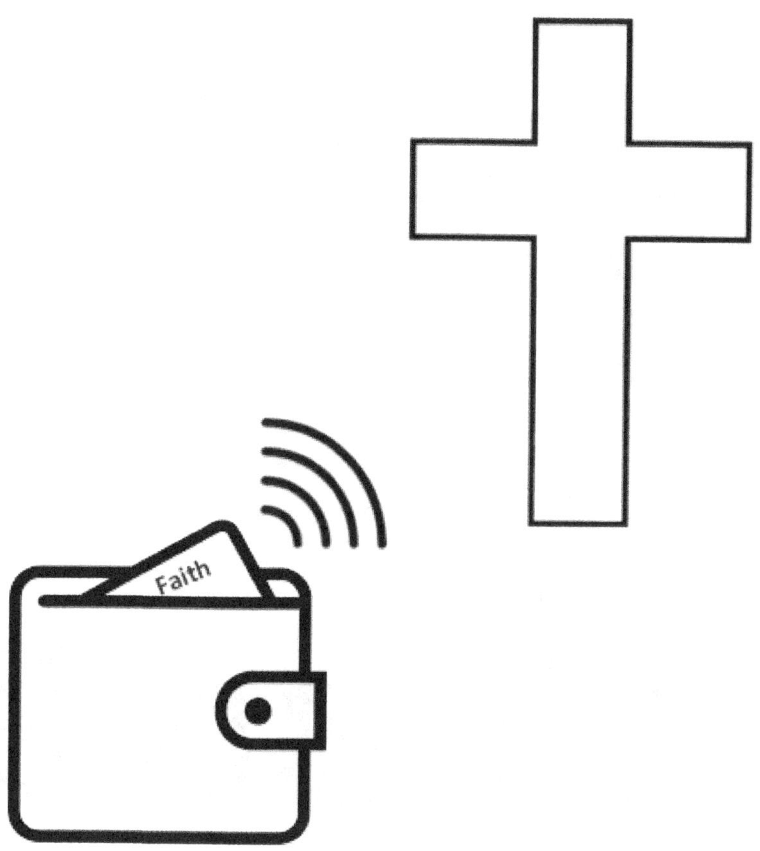

"Faith is the currency of heaven… *What's in your wallet?"*

Kayon Rodney

Faith
&
WORKS

CHAPTER 4

FINANCIALLY SPEAKING: *The right mindset*

"You seem to think that money grows on trees!"

Sounds familiar? Anyone?

Of course it does!

That's one variation of the famous "age-old" line that parents and guardians often use in response to requests made on them by their children (young and old). This is usually accompanied by furrowed brows and incredulous (and sometimes annoyed) facial expressions. It doesn't matter what part of the world we are from, at some point or another, most of us have had some variation of this line used on us as children and young adults. Oftentimes it's in response to requests that parents don't consider to be a "need" or worse, it's in response to an irresponsible action that will result in unnecessary spending.

This just got me thinking...

With the emergence of this new trend of buying and gifting "money trees", wouldn't it be just amusingly cheeky to point out (during one of these opportune moments) that there are in fact such trees? "*Money trees!*"

Disclaimer:

I claim no responsibility for any resulting actions which might come from your "pointing this out"... *especially if your parents are of Caribbean, Asian or African descent.*

Do so at your own risk!

COUNTING THE COSTS

Seriously speaking though, money tree or not, money does not grow on trees. This painful reality hits home for many during their college years. Those years when ***every dollar counts and is NEEDED***. Where a few dollars short could be the difference between:

- *starting a course of study or deferring;*
- *continuing studies or dropping out;*
- *registering for courses or being barred from doing so or from sitting exams;*

- *a place to sleep or out on the streets;*
- *food to eat or going hungry; or*
- *completing a degree or becoming part of the statistic of broken and unfulfilled dreams of higher education*

You name it...

The truth is, for persons living outside of countries where education is free or highly subsidized up to the tertiary level, the cost of tertiary education can be quite expensive. So expensive, that most students (not all) struggle to finance their way through college, or resort to less than morally acceptable or admirable activities to fund this venture.

For most college students, financially speaking, "*the struggle is real*!" While I would love to tell you that once you're a Christian then you won't face financial woes in college, that would be a most vicious lie. Being a Christian guarantees that you are saved from the wages of sin (death), not exempt from the challenges of life.

> **Being a Christian guarantees that you are saved from the wages of sin (death),** not exempt from the challenges of life.
>
> **With every challenge** however, **God provides** what is needed to endure and overcome.

So don't get blindsided into thinking that Christians are exempt from financial challenges in college. They're not.

Matter of fact, for many Christians in college and facing financial challenges, another category gets added to the "*difference between*" list highlighted before. The difference between:

- *maintaining Godly principles and values or compromising to make ends meet.*

Let's not kid ourselves... we know this is one of the white elephants in the graduation gown. The fact that many students (Christians and non-Christians) compromise moral, ethical and spiritual values in their efforts at "making ends meet" while in college.

For example, the stories abound of students who have "slept" (and are sleeping) their way through university. In plain "naked elephant" terms, these students exchange sex (and other associated acts) for money to pay their way through college. And that is just one of the more infamous methods that some students have resorted to out of desperation. There are many others too; for example, stealing, selling assignments, selling prohibited drugs, sex for grades and so on.

Yes... the white elephant is now laid bare...

Naked for all to acknowledge.

This is one of the taboo topics that many speak about in hushed tones. This is done either for love of gossip and disdain of the practice, or regret at the "level" that some students have brought themselves to in an effort to secure "money" to fund their way through college.

Oftentimes, desperation causes students to feel backed into a corner, hedged in by the reality of ballooning tuitions, living expenses and so on, with limited or depleted resources. This issue of limited or depleted resources may be due to changes in circumstances between the time they started their course of study and its progression, or just being in a financially challenging period or season. For example, some students might have started out with financial support from parents, family, friends, scholarships, student loans and so on. However, at some point for some, their revenue stream dries up. This may be due to job losses, death of the financier, grades falling below the "agreed upon" GPA or any of several reasons.

Of course, desperation kicks in as several see their goals in sight but perceive the daunting financial obstacles in the way. Added to this is the dreaded perception of missing their opportunity at a better life and returning or resorting to a life of broken and unfulfilled dreams - as may be evident in their families and communities. Therefore, many jump at "compromise" clothed as opportunity. After all... *"It's just a means to an end, and I'll have my degree at the end."* This is one of the several thoughts that may cross the minds of some students as they seek to rationalize the decision to secure funding through various morally suspect and sinful means.

Desperation is a known precursor to compromise...

However, let me quickly add:

No degree is worth the expense of compromising Godly standards.

NONE!

Therefore, be careful of the thoughts, plans, and actions conceived and executed during moments or periods of desperation. The Bible reminds us to be on guard against desperation and its relatives - anxiety and impulsive actions. *See* ***Philippians 4:6-7 (ESV):***

"Do not be anxious about anything, but in everything by prayer and supplication with thanksgiving let your requests be made known to God. And the peace of God, which surpasses all understanding, will guard your hearts and your minds in Christ Jesus."

This "anything" includes how we view our financial situations, no matter how CHALLENGING they may seem.

GOD IS ABLE!!!

One thing is certain, and that is that God always works everything for good, even the challenges (financial and otherwise). After all, the Bible tells us in **Romans 8:28**, that *"...all things work together for good, to them that love God, to them who are called according to His purpose."* That's the Word of God and it never lies!

You can bank on that... no pun intended.

Christians in college are called to "trust" beyond what they might be seeing as financial challenges and impossibilities. This takes faith...

> "... *the substance of things hoped for, the evidence of things not seen.*" ***Hebrews 11:1***

What you may be seeing as a recipe for failure, desperation and possible compromise, might just be the chosen platform for God to perform a miracle in your life. One that you'll testify of for years to come. *Don't allow desperation to taint or steal your testimony.*

> **What you may be seeing as a recipe for failure, desperation and possible compromise,** might just be the chosen platform for God to perform a miracle in your life.
>
> ***Don't allow desperation to taint or steal your testimony.***

FAITH, WORKS AND WISDOM IN FINANCES

Wouldn't you just love if you prayed and asked God for financial provision, then opened your eyes and...

Poof!!

A stack of cash, "bow wrapped" right by your feet!

OR

An actual money tree, with real money that gets replenished each time you pick a few bills!

Like yea...

Somewhere out there, that happens!

Somewhere...

For example... In cartoons for sure!

In reality, however, it doesn't quite work that way.

Nope... It does not.

While it does not work that way however, God has innumerable natural and supernatural ways of providing for your needs, including those concerned with finances. He is ***ABLE*** and ***CAPABLE***, and it is ***POSSIBLE***.

You do not need to compromise Godliness to "make ends meet" while in college.

There are ways to successfully navigate the financial challenges of the college period while maintaining Godly principles.

Here's how:

Faith

Works

Wisdom

Be persistent in faith and prayer. Ensure at all times that you support your prayers with "works" & by extension, wisdom. In other words, after praying for financial sustenance, have faith that God can and will do it, then find ways to walk out that faith in practical actions.

Do not be caught harbouring "dead faith".

The Bible tells us that faith and works go hand-in-hand and that faith without the requisite works (actions and dispositions which support what you believe to be true) is dead (*read James 2:14-26).*

Don't just stop at praying.

Put your faith into action

So, even as you pray and trust that God will grant you favour and successful financial passage throughout the college journey, do not neglect to implement the "works" aspect as much as possible.

Now before we go any further, let's agree on a working definition of "works" in light of our discussion. Think of "works" broadly (in this context) to include any action taken to aid or support financial wisdom through acquiring and managing money and resources. Don't limit your thoughts of "works" to just the natural sense of "paid labour or service".

Equally, any discussion about the right mindset in faith and finances must also lay the foundation for cultivating the right attitude, eventually manifesting in the appropriate actions. After all, before God blesses us, He has to prepare us. This preparation is meant to ensure our heart's posture is right and our actions follow suit. Therefore, as you pray for, and pursue financial sustenance in college, keep a constant check on your attitude and actions regarding God's provision.

THE RIGHT ATTITUDE

This is first and foremost, yet most often overlooked...

The story is often told of a gentleman who felt he was at the end of his rope. As he looked at his life, he became more and more despondent at the daily state of lack that he had to endure. All around him others seemed to be having easier lives, prospering and having all the "good things", yet here he was, working extremely hard but rarely ever able to make ends meet. The more he thought on the matter, the more depressed he became.

Convinced that he could no longer carry on in the life of poverty that he was living, he decided to end his life. Climbing a tree, he sat on a limb and took a ripe banana from his pocket, his last meal before ending his life. After taking the last bite of his last meal, he threw the banana peel to the ground below.

Within seconds of hitting the ground, the peel was quickly snatched up by a homeless man who happened to be passing beneath the tree at that exact moment. Banana peel in hand, the homeless man then lifted his hands to the heavens and gave thanks to God before quickly consuming the peel. The man in the tree above was dumbstruck, ashamed and heartbroken all at once! He suddenly realized that no matter how bad it seemed, there is always much to be thankful for. Further, there were persons more challenged than he was, yet more grateful. How truly ungrateful he felt!

In case you're wondering...

No, he did not end his life after that encounter.

Instead, he learnt the lesson, to be grateful in all things.

On that note...

Be grateful for what you have

When was the last time you thanked God for all that you have?

I mean really thanked Him! You know... not the surface thanks with little depth, but rather, a deep heartfelt thanks which stems from a heart of gratitude. A heart that sees God's provision in all that it has, instead of one blindsided by all that it doesn't have. God honours a grateful heart. The Bible tells us in **Psalm 100:4** that we should:

"Enter into His gates with thanksgiving, and into His courts with praise: be thankful unto Him and bless His name."

Gratitude and praise get you through the gate and into His courts. Therefore, I would dare say that without these two, you are locked out of His presence, and by extension His blessings. Practice approaching God with a heart of gratitude as this is a crucial aspect of entering into His presence.

> **Practice approaching God with a heart of gratitude.**
> Gratitude and praise get you through the gate and into God's courts. Without these two, you are locked out of His presence, and by extension His blessings

So, things might not be the way you want them to be right now, but there is always much to be thankful for. The timeless hymn reminds us to:

Count your blessings, name them one by one;
Count your blessings, see what God hath done;
Count your blessings, name them one by one;
Count your many blessings, see what God hath done.

How do you do this?

Well...

Even before you approach God making requests, take the time to think about everything you can thank Him for. As you practice doing so, suddenly you start to realize just how many things there are to be grateful for. This attitude of gratitude will automatically cause you to be in awe of God's love and provision. *So much so, that this can sometimes cause you to forget what you intended to request of Him.* Equally, this will increase your faith to trust God to provide what you need at this stage of your journey.

After all...

Being grateful also serves as a reminder that the same God who has been providing, is aware of your needs at present and will provide according to His will.

So…

The next time you feel tempted to overlook that ripe banana in hand, remember that there is someone out there who would be grateful for even 10% of what you have.

Be grateful!

THE RIGHT ACTIONS

Would you take your hard-earned money and keep giving it to someone whom you know will not spend it wisely? Someone who will just "blow it" on any and everything that tickles his or her fancy, with no consideration for prioritizing needs over wants?

Equally, and along that same line of reasoning…

Be a good steward!

Can God trust you to be a good financial steward?

- How are you with your finances?
- Do you squander money?
- Do you spend frivolously?
- Are you always borrowing for unnecessary purchases?
- Do you spend above that which you are able to comfortably maintain?

- Do you spend within your means or more within your "impulses and desires?"
- Do you exercise prudence in the handling of your financial affairs?

It doesn't matter if it is hundreds, thousands, millions or billions, your financial track record is crucial to any conversation regarding financial management. This entails your ability to: prioritize, plan and control spending habits, live within your means, and set and stick to financial goals.

On that note...

How is your financial track record?

For many young persons in college, this is the first time they are (or will be) making financial decisions without the constant oversight or control of parents and guardians. For others, however, they might have a bit more financial management experience through work and otherwise, and thus would have the added advantage of being better prepared to effectively handle their finances while in college. Regardless of experience or not, everyone needs to be good stewards of their finances while in college, and even beyond.

God expects us to exercise wisdom in all things. This also includes how we handle our finances. Therefore, practice wise financial management. Here are two foundational tips that can help you in this regard, even as you seek to be a good steward of that which God has already allowed you to possess.

✓ *Exercise self-control*

Not everything that you want is worth purchasing, and especially not always at the time you might be considering. If you can reasonably foresee that making a particular unnecessary purchase would result in a shortfall in an area which is considered a "need", then resist the urge. Don't put yourself in a position of discomfort caused by trying to make up the shortfall in your budget due to unnecessary spending.

For example, it is probably not the best decision to splurge on brand-name earbuds if it will come at the expense of you dipping into the money that is set aside for making a payment on your tuition, or money set aside for purchasing food for the month. Avoid making impulsive purchases. Stick to your budget as much as possible and *PRIORITIZE!*

✓ *Budget... budget... budget!*

Create a realistic budget and stick to it. Be sure to review and update your budget regularly so it is always reflective of your current circumstances as well as the changes in the cost of living and associated expenses. There are tons of resources online that can help with creating a budget that works for you.

Google and put one together.

Budgets help you to live within your means as you know in advance what you are able to spend without finding yourself in the red zone. With your budget in hand, the next step is to exercise self-control and learn to live within your means.

The fact of the matter is...

Finances are usually "tight" for most college students. However, this is never a justifiable excuse for compromising Godliness to "make ends meet" – tempting as it might be. Therefore, when faced with financial difficulties, choose to look ahead through the eyes of faith as supported by works and wisdom. Be persistent in faith, works and prayer, while trusting that God will work out any and all financial challenges that you may face, according to His will. And even as you pursue financial provision, cultivate a mindset of financial prudence and wise money management, undergirded by a heart of gratitude.

With this foundation laid, let's move on to the next chapter where we will explore in more detail, some practical strategies, tips and programmes that are available to help students fund and manage college expenses. These avenues of financial support are crucial for promoting and supplementing your financial stability throughout college.

LET'S REFLECT!

Having read this chapter, what are some important points that you'd like to note?

Note to self...

"Don't just stop at praying, pursue financial opportunities relentlessly through persistent faith and works."

Kayon Rodney

it is

~~im~~possible

CHAPTER 5

FUNDING & MANAGING COLLEGE EXPENSES

Where is the wealthy long lost (never met) uncle who upon his death, left a will with specific instructions to have all your college tuition and expenses paid throughout your period of study?

"That uncle" seems to have skipped over many families. I'll take a guess and say that he probably skipped your family too.

Yup! skipped right over...

The truth is that for most students, college doesn't exactly come fully paid for upfront - whether through a rich family member or otherwise. This fact, therefore, makes it ever so crucial to have a plan in place regarding ways you can supplement or access sufficient financial resources and support to take you through your period of study. For many persons, this may mean pulling on one, several or all of the support systems and options which will be explored in this chapter.

Whatever method or methods chosen, of course, should be implemented in conjunction with the sound financial management tips as outlined in the previous chapter.

Long lost, wealthy uncle aside...

> *It is possible to successfully complete your degree without compromising your Godly principles and character to "make ends meet" financially. Many have done it. So can you.*

Here's how:

Utilize the myriad of financial support systems available to college students to aid them in funding their college expenses. Some of these options might not be feasible for all students. However, I guarantee that before you have come to the end of this chapter, you would have identified several avenues and strategies that you can utilize in funding and managing your college expenses.

So, l*et's explore some of these.*

1 FAMILY AND FRIENDS

Family and friends form two of the main support systems for most students in college, especially those who enter college right out of high school. This support may be in the form of paying tuition and other related costs or acting as guarantors for securing the requisite student loans.

Even with family and friends footing the bill, however, this does not negate the need for personal responsibility. If for nothing else, then from a place of gratitude for their sacrifice, support and commitment towards helping you to achieve your dreams. This requires that you still exercise due financial prudence with whatever resources they might provide you with, weekly, monthly or whatever timeframe.

Even with a seemingly secured source of funding, always consider a plan B.

PLAN B

Another important aspect which I would urge you to consider is a plan B. Always entertain a plan B which will put you one step ahead.

What do I mean?

Well, let's say something happens and the person or persons who were funding your college expenses are no longer able to do so. What do you do then? Having a plan B, considers, even to a small extent, the "what if". So, for example, the main financier of your education loses his or her job and the financing of your education is severely affected, what do you do in the immediate aftermath? What are some steps you could take to continue your schooling?

While you can never plan for all eventualities, having a "*what if*" mindset will see you looking at options in advance, even if it turns out that you might never need to resort to plan B. A good addition to your plan B mindset is developing a habit of saving from whatever you might be receiving, no matter how small.

> **Always consider your plan B.** Your "What if" option.
>
> A "what if" mindset will see you looking at options in advance, even if it turns out that you might never need to resort to plan B.
>
> **It doesn't hurt...**

So, research other options of funding & supplementing your finances in case it becomes necessary (for example, through part-time jobs, payment plans, grants and so on). Better to be prepared and never need to use plan B than to be taken by surprise and without a possible plan B.

2 PART-TIME JOBS

Part-time jobs are not only for plan Bs.

Matter of fact, holding down part-time jobs are plans A, B, C and D for many college students who are studying full-time. This is a vital lifeline that many students utilize to be able to study while earning or vice versa. These jobs are often available ***on or off campus*** in various areas. In fact, most universities and colleges actually employ students in part-time positions to work on campus.

With the proliferation of technology, another avenue has also opened for helping to supplement finances while in college; the rise of ***online jobs and freelance work***. These can be easily accessed by researching online and consulting freelance sites such as FIVERR, where persons (including college students) offer their services in many different areas to potential clients from all over the world. These jobs range from low to high-skilled, short or long-term stints or projects.

In addition, there are also options such as those afforded by ***summer jobs and internships***. Many private and government agencies gladly welcome students to fill summer job positions and internships. However, these are quite competitive and are best applied for early (before summer break begins). Look out for these jobs as soon as they are advertised and apply... apply...

For students, especially those from the Caribbean and studying at a university or college, "***work and travel" programmes*** also provide another helpful source of gathering finances. With these programmes, students are able to travel overseas and gain employment for the summer then return home to continue their studies after the summer break. This is one of the preferred options utilized by several college students to fund their studies.

However, a word of caution is especially important here...

Not all work and travel programmes are created equal!

There have been many horror stories from students of having been scammed by purported job agencies or having been provided jobs that required them to work in inhumane conditions and worse for mere pittance. Therefore, it is advised that you exercise caution if you choose to embark on this route to finance or supplement your college expenses.

Research... research... and research before making your decisions.

A good place to start this research is by contacting the Student Affairs office of your college as well as talking to other students who have gone on the "work and travel" programme.

On or off campus work, online, summer jobs, or work and travel programs... these all form part of the part-time job portfolio that are available to help students in college maintain financial stability and fund their tertiary education.

It must be noted however, that the pursuit of part-time employment must be carefully considered with a view to finding the right balance between financial pursuits and maintaining the required academic standards. If not handled properly, many students can find themselves falling behind in school as they struggle to keep up with the overwhelming workloads which come with having one or more part-time jobs.

Equally, care must be given to ensuring that one is getting adequate sleep.

"A*dequate sleep in college..."*

Mmmphh...

Sounds like an oxymoron if ever there was one, but, even so, *adequate sleep is crucial.*

It surely would not be beneficial to have sufficient finances, but insufficient sleep and the associated ills of falling behind or failing courses, or worse, declining health and immune system. That would be counter-productive quite frankly. So, ensure that you strike the right balance in these matters if you are considering or are already pursuing part-time job opportunities while studying.

3 SCHOLARSHIPS, GRANTS & BURSARIES

Scholarships, grants and bursaries!! These avenues of financial support are seen as "God-sent" for students in college!

While differing in their reasons for being awarded and their administration and requirements, these three concepts stem from the same foundation: *monies given which you do not have to repay.*

The following table provides a quick comparison for ease of reference.

<table>
<tr><td colspan="3"><u>Scholarships</u>
Financial assistance awarded to students by different organizations for various reasons, such as:</td></tr>
<tr><td>- Financial need</td><td>- Academic merit</td><td>- Athletic achievement</td></tr>
<tr><td>- Talent in various areas</td><td>- Business promotion</td><td>- To boost enrolment in select areas of study eg. STEM</td></tr>
<tr><td colspan="3"><u>Bursaries and Grants</u>
These are usually given to students who meet specific “financial needs” or qualifying criteria; such as “underrepresented” groups or areas of study. For example:</td></tr>
<tr><td>- Students suffering financial hardship</td><td>- Students with disabilities</td><td>- Students from low-income homes</td></tr>
</table>

Source: Scholarshiphub.org (2022)

There are also other requirements that may be necessary for accessing these means of support. For example, the requirement that students have and maintain a specified minimum GPA. *This is most often the case.* In addition, some may require that students perform mandated minimum hours of voluntary work or community service as part of additional requirements for qualifying for these benefits.

Well worth trade-offs in my opinion...

While the information I have provided is general, different scholarships, bursaries and grants always outline their specific requirements and proposed disbursements in advance. This entails what are the overall requirements necessary for applicants to be favourably considered, the value of the proposed financial assistance and what it is intended to cover. The most common areas covered include; offsetting tuition fees (full, half, or other percentage-based support), living expenses, as well as books and other related allocations. Equally, these scholarships and grants may cover all or part of a student's college-associated expenses for part of their study or for the entire duration.

As varied as the scholarships and grants are, so too are the sources from which they can be accessed. These sources can be categorized under several headings, such as; charitable organizations, school alumni, private businesses and government ministries and agencies and agents.

If approved for financial assistance, the monies from these programmes are almost always paid over to the school directly, rather than into the student's personal bank account.

So... there goes your immediate dreams of a "fat" bank account if even for a few hours or days.

Unlikely to happen this way!

Not that that should matter much! It is the financial assistance that is needed to complete your studies, not so much being able to access the actual money.

With that being said...

PERSISTENT FAITH AND WORKS...

I witnessed firsthand the value of these avenues of funding in the lives of many college students. One of my Christian classmate's experiences however, stood far out above the rest. The entire four years of her studies (full-time) were made possible through funding received from private and public grants and scholarships. I reckon that approximately 98% of her fees were paid through these avenues. So much so, that she left college debt free!

No student loans! Not owing anyone! Paid for in full!

Did I also mention that this was while she was juggling being a single parent of 3 boys, and without a steady stream of income?

Yea... that happened!

Of course, she would be the first to tell you that it was all due to God's faithfulness and I totally agree! I would also hasten to add that it was God's faithfulness and her trust in His promises, that propelled her to put that faith into action.

Things did not magically fall into her lap!

She believed that God could and would. This propelled her to remain steadfast in faith and prayer as well as employ wisdom to research and apply for available grants and scholarships. Over and over too, as she did not get one or two scholarships to fund her studies throughout. *Nope.* Year by year, semester by semester, she would meticulously hunt down the opportunities and apply by faith. Some she was successful at, others not so much, but she persevered.

She also refused to take "*no*" for an answer from any human opposition when they tried to convince her to defer her studies until she could afford to comfortably meet the financial requirements. *Not that there is anything wrong with deferring, if necessary, as this is an option that many students have utilized and eventually resumed to successfully complete their studies.* However, as she would adamantly point out, "God already told me "*Yes,* and that the time is now*!*" Therefore, if one door was closed, she knocked on another two or three. One or more had to open! And opened they did!

God said it, she believed it, and acted by faith!

What about you?

Can you also exercise persistent faith?

God is not partial, so He can do it for you as well. The avenues are there. It is for you to align with the requirements and pursue the opportunities by faith, trusting God to work things out for good according to His will. Don't just stop at praying, pursue the opportunities.

Here's how:

Research, network, apply!

One of the first steps is researching the available scholarships, grants and bursaries for your field of study, age group, college, parish, province, state, country, region and so on. Any or all of those variations. This should provide you with a pretty extensive list!

Don't just stop at praying, pursue the opportunities.

- Research
- Network
- Apply yourself

Some avenues of support include **family & friends, part-time jobs, student loans, payment plans, scholarships & so on...**

Start with your college campus student affairs office or department. It should be able to provide you with a listing of scholarships, grants and bursaries available to students as well as provide general timelines and guidelines as to when they open and what are the general requirements.

This of course is sufficient information to get you started with preparing to apply. Part of the pre-application process then includes doing further research on each opportunity to ascertain specific information and apprise yourself of requirements which might not have been covered by the Student Affairs department. This information you can find by doing online research as well as contacting the responsible parties and offices in charge of granting these scholarships (by telephone, email or even in person if possible).

In addition, network with other students on campus. Chances are they know of scholarship opportunities or know of someone who has accessed financial assistance from various sources. These referrals provide a wealth of information that can help to guide you in your research and access to financial opportunities.

Another useful avenue is signing up for notifications on websites that track scholarship and grant opportunities. Along that same line, utilize these online platforms to conduct research into the available avenues of financial assistance available to students in your region, country and field of study.

Be proactive and persistent. It pays off!

4 PAYMENT PLANS

Many students opt for payment plans for the obvious reason; the benefit it provides of easing the financial pressures of finding thousands of dollars upfront all at once. With the tuition broken into smaller and 'more manageable' portions, students are able to continue studying while saving and working towards paying the next tranche of their tuition when it becomes due.

A payment plan, in this case, is an agreement between a student and the college that the student will pay specified amounts at varying intervals until the expenses are cleared. This is a route that many students choose as a more manageable means of paying the costs of their college education. Many colleges and universities offer students various payment plans with intervals such as per semester, per credit, and payment of tuitions in halves or thirds. Of course, tuitions paid through payment plan methods are usually slightly more expensive in the long run as most institutions add interest as part of the payment plan. However, for the ease that payment plans provide, the added interest does not diminish or outweigh the overarching benefits.

Also...

Watch those terms, conditions and deadlines!

Based on the payment plan agreed upon, students are expected to abide by the terms and conditions as well as pay on or before each deadline. The consequences of failing to abide by payment deadlines are often rigid and range from being barred from registering for courses and exams to even being deregistered from your programme of study.

It is important to note that there are also often rigid requirements that all outstanding fees for previous semesters be cleared in full before students are allowed to register for upcoming exams or progress to another year of study.

Unfortunately...

Most colleges do not play the "carry forward" game very well.

So, here's some advice:

Consider this option if necessary. The benefits of entering into a payment plan agreement for paying your fees far outweigh the disadvantages. If you need further information on available payment plans at your college, contact your student affairs office or the college's accounting department. Either of these offices will be able to assist by directing you to the appropriate department and forms which you will need to complete in order to apply for a payment plan.

Please note however...

One, you must try as best as possible to abide by the terms of your payment plan if you have entered into one, as your "*payment plan*" footprint will either assist you in being approved for, or denied access to further payment plan agreements with the college. In this case as well... *your reputation precedes you.*

Two, use the period in between payments wisely. If you have a payment plan agreement with your college, do not become comfortable or complacent after making a payment. Immediately start stockpiling money towards the next payment, even if it is a few months away. You would be surprised to see how fast time flies, especially when it comes to paying monies due on a payment plan. Avoid the last-minute rush and associated anxiety as much as it is within your power to do so. Equally, if you find yourself with some "unexpected money", how about paying some down on your tuition, even before the next payment becomes due?

It certainly doesn't hurt!

Consider this:

When it comes on to payment plans, be like a squirrel on a mad dash stockpiling nuts for winter.

Grab every nut you can. Start gathering early!

Winter is always on the horizon and every nut, well,

every dollar, counts!

5 STUDENT LOANS

A student loan in its simplest sense, is a loan offered to students by government or private businesses such as banks and credit unions. Here are some interesting facts on student loans for you. In the U.S, for example:

- *"Student loan debt is the second highest category of debt – second only to mortgage loans.*
- *Among adults with student loan debt, 93% report borrowing to pay for their own education while 81% report borrowing to pay for a child's or grandchild's education.*
- *94.8% of people with student loan debt borrowed for an undergraduate education."*

Statistics source: *"Student loan statistics"* by Melanie Hanson. (April, 2022). https://educationdata.org/student-loan-debt-statistics

Similarly, in several countries around the world, student loans provide a vital source through which students receive funding for tertiary education. These types of loans cover college expenses, allowing recipients to complete their tertiary studies before they have to begin repaying the loan. While that has been the traditional route, repaying the loan while you study is also available for students who choose this option.

Wait... there's a catch!

With most student loans however, there is the requirement for students (borrowers) to provide one or more guarantors as part of qualifying for such a loan. This guarantor is a person or persons who agree to repay the loan in the event that the student defaults on repaying the loan. And that is the catch! Finding persons to act as guarantors, of course, has often posed a challenge for many students, as many times possible guarantors are either unwilling or incapable of meeting the guarantor requirements as outlined by the lending institutions.

However, if a willing and suitable guarantor is identified, then three-quarters of the potential challenges are over. The rest is left up to providing the necessary documentation and undertakings as may be required by the proposed lender.

As there is no one size fits all loan, it is left up to individual students or their parents and guardians, to research the most suitable loan for their situation and how to go about accessing same. Two good places to start this research are online, and the student affairs department of the prospective college or the college that the student currently attends. Through these avenues, you will be able to find relevant information to help guide you in the process of successfully applying for a student loan

6 CHURCH COMMUNITY

While not a traditional route of assistance for studies, some church communities might be able and willing to provide occasional or one-off assistance for college expenses.

Now hold your horses...

Don't start watching the offering basket or plate thinking you are entitled to "college help" from this source as you are a member.

This kind of help is left to the discretion of your church and may be based on several factors such as their ability to afford to provide even a one-off assistance at the moment. Of course, this is not a guarantee, nor a benefit for which you "apply". This avenue is mentioned more along the lines of being a "possible" option. An option whereby you could approach your church community to ascertain if it might be able to offer assistance, no matter how minuscule or infrequent it might be - if at all. Even while doing so, be sure to keep your expectations in check as they might not be able to offer any assistance based on various reasons. After all...

It's not like the church has a revolving "common college fund" that you have been paying into...

Just thought I'd put that out there for clarity.

Clarity aside, your church community is a potential source of occasional assistance. You may go about this option by penning a letter to the appropriate leadership board seeking assistance. It will then respond by letting you know if it is able to or not, or as the case may be.

Success rides on the back of planning and executing the requisite financial pathways with wisdom. This is also true of funding and managing your expenses in college and beyond. College can be quite an expensive venture. However, there are various options which offer invaluable sources that can be maximized to help you pay your way through college. Therefore, don't just stop at praying, pursue these opportunities relentlessly through persistent faith and works.

It is possible!

LET'S REFLECT!

Having read this chapter, what are some important points that you'd like to note?

Note to self...

"It looks, [feels] and sounds good, but is it God?"

Pastor Musa Laing

HAVE

Consulted

God ?

CHAPTER 6

#RELATIONSHIP.GOALS

Readiness For Dating

LOVE is in air!

Scratch that! Let me rephrase…

"LUST and INFATUATION, with an occasional whiff of love" is in the air… wear your mask!

Be careful what you are breathing in.

Beneath the academic and social atmosphere lies extremely active and pervading scenes featuring lust, infatuation and occasional appearances by love. With the main cast, naturally, being made up of students from all year groups seemingly vying for a space in the movie. Of course, this is against the backdrop of many persons getting carried along with the ebb and flow of mostly short-lived flings or "hook-ups", driven mainly by lust and infatuation. The fact of the matter is that there are extensively more failed "relationships" and "situationships" in college, when compared to the few that last and make it beyond graduation.

Like the desire for "passing grades", in college, the pursuit of the "feel-good effect" from being in an intimate relationship is never far away. Therefore, many rush headlong into "casual" relationships and sex, just for the purpose of "looking" and "feeling" good and "fitting in" with the crowd and culture. Of course, there is never any thought about the Godly requirements and purposes for getting close to another person in an intimate relationship.

This is not strange however, as the world has many ungodly guidelines which it incessantly promotes overtly and covertly through songs, movies, magazines and every other imaginable avenue. These all promote the idea that,

> *Hey!*
> *It is ok to fulfil sexual desires with whatever gender tickles your fancy, through one-night stands, flings, friends with benefits, casual romances, dating relationships...* You name it.

It doesn't help either, that the college experience itself has been explicitly and implicitly marketed by movies and songs, as a time of wanton exploring, experimenting and testing the waters; chief of which includes engaging in sexually immoral behaviours, drinking and drugs.

So, of course, it is almost a natural progression when many people enter college, for them to follow suit on the subliminal messages they have been exposed to in these movies and songs. In addition, college is often the first real taste of independence for many young persons. Their first opportunity to come and go, as well as do as they desire, being away from the watchful eyes of family and for some, the church community.

Newfound freedom plus low accountability and pressures from the pervading college culture, many times result in a fueling of the desire to discard all reservations and engage in wanton behaviour with reckless abandon. This is almost seen as a rite of passage of the college experience.

> Wanton and sexually immoral behaviours are almost seen as a rite of passage in college.
>
> **Rite,** however**, does not make it right,** no more than "looking and feeling good" makes it God.

The Bible tells us in **Proverbs 14:12** that, "there is a way that seems right to a man, but its end is the way of death" (NKJV). It is truly interesting how creative persons often become as they attempt to justify sin. For example, take the thoughts that flutter through persons' heads as they try to justify their pursuit and engagement in drinking, drugs, and sexually immoral behaviours while in college:

This is just for a period of time anyways!

I'm just experimenting a little.

I'm exercising my independence and freedom!

Most persons are doing the same thing so what....

What happens in college stays in college!

Sadly, this is not a snare that only captures unbelievers; several Christians get carried away with this mindset in college. Many openly or secretly embrace this "free reign" culture and are led away by their own lusts and fleshly desires - drowning out the protests of the Spirit. The result is that they also engage in meaningless relationships and flings, to satisfy their own fleshly desires of "looking" and "feeling" good. Of course, in attempting to sweep this under the rug, they stifle their consciences with the excuses above plus this one:

No one from back home (family or church) will ever find out, and once this college experience is over, I leave this season and its shenanigans behind.

How about God though...

Doesn't He know?

Or will He also get left behind along with the season?

SEX AND SEXUALITY

In college especially, the issue of sex and sexuality is never far away. Whether it is through advised or ill-advised dating, lustful pursuits, curious conversations and encounters or promiscuous activities. Whatever the serving, it is important that you have a full grasp and understanding of the Godly principles surrounding these topics. It is this understanding that will help to guard against falling victim to the culture of sexual immorality that is present in most colleges. With the vastness and complexity of this subject however, where does one begin?

Well...

Maybe at the beginning?

In the beginning...

The question comes forth:

Is it normal to have sexual feelings as a Christian?

This is one of many unvoiced questions of several young Christians, and the simple and quick answer is...

YES!

Many young Christians struggle with questions about their sexuality, and how to reconcile these in practical ways with their faith. *The truth is*, except for the passionate sermons against fornication as issued from the pulpit, many do not have an avenue to ask questions or benefit from discussions about sex and sexuality from the church's perspective.

Sex is often seen as a taboo topic, and one which is only touched by those leaders and churches that have come to the correct realization, that young Christians need practical guidance on this issue. They need proper and practical guidance about sex and sexuality in order to avoid falling prey to the alluring temptations and pitfalls of sexual immorality.

Sexual feelings and desires...

Understand that people do not exist in unfeeling bubbles, and this also includes Christians. The last time I checked, Christians are people too! We have the same biological inclinations as other persons. So yes, we are capable of having sexual desires and feeling physically and sexually attracted to other persons – this is quite normal. In fact, Paul the Apostle alludes to this in **1 Corinthians 7:9**,

Feeling sexually attracted to the opposite sex is not a sin. However, it is a sin to fixate on these desires (lust) or act on them outside of marriage.

Bring your sexual desires under subjection using the Word of God.

encouraging unmarried and widowed persons that if they are unable to control themselves (their sexual desires), then it is better to marry than burn with passions.

So yea, passions and sexual attractions do not magically appear after one gets married. They are natural biological processes, which in and of themselves are not sin. They cross over into the realm of sin when we choose to fixate on them in the act of lustful thoughts; as well as allow these thoughts to lead us into physically acting on them outside of the sanctity of marriage (masturbation, fornication and so on).

As a Christian, *you are not called to be ashamed of your sexuality*, but rather to bring your desires (sexual and otherwise) under subjection using the Word of God to guide your decisions.

If I had a dollar for every time I heard this!

"Bring your body under subjection..."

Like...

How do I bring my body under subjection though?

Practically speaking...

How does this look?

In case your mind went off the deep end again, projecting images of literally "anointing" your body with a physical Bible, let me help you out here. *Nothing quite so dramatic actually.* In practical terms, you apply the Word of God to regulate and bring your thoughts and actions under control so that they line up with the Word of God.

For example, your perfectly ripped, totally hot crush from the track team walks by and there goes your eyes, head and thoughts! In rushes those inappropriate sexual thoughts, racing at breakneck speed towards lust!

Stop them in their tracks!

No pun intended...

You had better quickly erect those roadblocks in the form of Bible verses such as **Philippians 4:8,** *"whatsoever things are pure, whatsoever things are lovely, whatsoever things are of good report; if there be any virtue, and if there be any praise, think on these things."* Don't just stop there either! Keep forcefully presenting the Word of God to your mind. Flood your mind with those scriptures that encourage pure thoughts and warn against lust, even while reaffirming that you will not allow your flesh and its sinful desires to cause you to rebel against God. Keep doing this until the lustful thoughts have subsided. Equally, exercise care and responsibility in your actions. Do not knowingly put yourself into situations which could lead to compromising results.

The Bible tells us to resist the enemy and he will flee!

Send the enemy and his immoral thoughts and actions packing!

This persistent "bringing your body under subjection" should not be a ritualistic practice either, but rather a response from a heart that loves God and wants to obey His commands. At the heart of the matter is *love and relationship with God over lust and rebellion against His commands.*

Bringing your body under subjection becomes even more pressing in college where many Christians face the pressure of the crowd to conform to the pervading sexually immoral practices. Being prepared to keep one's flesh under subjection is therefore a crucial element to consider for Christians in college, and especially for those desirous of dating.

Now that we have dealt with the basics of sex and sexuality, let's move on to look at dating readiness, from a Christian's viewpoint. As you read further, you will find useful insights and Biblical principles which you can wisely apply in navigating the dating scene.

READINESS FOR DATING – THE CHRISTIAN'S VIEWPOINT

So the "dating" bug comes along and everyone seems to be getting bitten. So much excitement and picture-perfect "*#Relationship Goals*" popping up across campus and on your social media pages. Oh, how the flesh might long for a bit of the fun and action that others seem to be having as they date. Remember, however…

Yes!

"It looks and sounds good, but is it God?" – Pastor Musa Laing.

So…

Is it the right time in your life for you to be dating?

Flesh aside; what is the Holy Spirit saying to you about dating at the moment? One of the most crucial steps that Christians need to take before asking someone on a date, or accepting an invitation for a date, is to identify whether or not they are ready for dating. Pray about it: ask the Holy Spirit.

Reason it out with God.

As with everything else, the decision to date or not to date should be based on Godly principles and motivations, and not the pervading culture of the world which focuses on what "feels" and "looks" good. We are in the world, but we are not of the world (**John 17:14-18**), and so worldly principles and guidelines should not be used as measuring instruments to dictate motivations, readiness or purpose for dating.

The decision to date or not to date should be based on Godly principles and motivations.

Worldly principles and guidelines should not be used as measuring instruments to dictate motivations, readiness or purpose for dating.

While the Bible does not explicitly address "dating" as a topic, it provides all the information necessary to help guide one's actions in the areas in between being single and married. Matter of fact, even beyond. The Bible is AMAZING like that!

Time to pointedly ask yourself, and answer this question:

<u>Am I ready to date?</u>

Before we go any further... those who are considering dating at the moment... pause for a minute and answer this question:

<u>Who are you?</u>

Are you still attempting to figure that out? As a rule of thumb, it certainly makes sense to first know who you are (your God-given identity) before seeking to present yourself to others or seeking to date. You cannot reasonably expect to offer yourself for someone to get to know you, when you don't even know yourself. Contrary to the worldly view that many subscribe to; you do not discover who you are through others. Remember, we dealt with this in chapters 1 and 2 of volume 1.

Next question...

Pause and think about this one as well, before responding.

<u>Why do you want to date?</u>

Now that you have answered that question, how close does your response align to this sentence? Dating in a Christian context is not mainly for frills and fun, but seeking a life partner who complements your purpose in God, even as you complement his or hers. Frills and fun do not dictate Christian compatibility. Don't get me wrong, there is nothing wrong with having fun while dating, matter of fact it is expected. However, those should be the accompaniments, not the main or sole goal.

Knowing who you are and establishing why you want to date are just two of the many factors that Christians should consider prior to dating.

> **Dating in a Christian context** should not be mainly for frills and fun, but **seeking a life partner who complements your purpose in God, even as you complement his or hers.**

Hindsight is 20/20 they say. I'll be the first to confess that when I started dating, those questions were nowhere near my thoughts, especially as an unsaved. It was all about the excitement and "feel good" effect for me. More of a pursuit to satisfy MY desires, which of course, often lead me down some ungodly paths. Add that to the fact that I was "dating" under an "assumed identity".

Assumed identity describes the fact that who I thought myself to be, was based on my past and present experiences and future desires - mostly ungodly of course. There was no consideration given to who God said I was and had called me to be.

Matter of fact, I didn't even know God, so there!

I lacked Godly direction, purpose, and even sufficient life experiences. This contributed to untold heartaches and hurtful mistakes, both to myself and others. Most of which I regret to this day, but I'm grateful to be able to use the lessons as testimonies to help others.

As I look back at the journey filled with instances of engaging in my own frolics, if it were at all possible, I would desperately shout to my past self:

"Girl! Danger up ahead!

You had better stop with all this foolishness and go submit to Christ!

Get saved and allow the Holy Spirit to direct your decisions!"

That's not all...

Were my past, stubborn self to listen and become saved, then at some point start considering dating, these are some of the frank questions I'd advise her to ask herself, before deciding to enter the dating scene. At this point, these questions are written for your benefit. After all, I can't very well direct my past self from the present, but these can certainly help to guide your decisions as a Christian considering dating.

Your responses to these questions will provide a general guideline as to whether or not you should even be considering dating, or need to spend more time allowing God to prepare you. Of course, we are all being perfected (**Philippians1:1-6**), so by no means am I suggesting that you have to be "perfect" to date.

If that were so, then you'd never end up dating!

Yet, while you nor I are perfect, we have to at least be actively engaged in the process of allowing Godly perfection to take its course. A course that will continue until Christ's return.

TWO VIEWS IN FIVE

I have presented two contradicting responses for each of the following 5 questions. Select the response under each that best reflects your current position or situation.

As you navigate these questions, if you are realizing that the majority of your responses are mostly aligned to the 2nd category of answers as against the first, this is an indication that there are too many red flags. In such a case, I encourage you to step back a little and seek God some more first. Work on yourself some more before making the decision to start dating. You don't need to rush.

So, here are the questions:

1 ***Do I have a firm grasp of who I am in Christ?***

- My identity is stable in Christ. I am not shaken when challenged on my identity. I both know and believe who God says I am and am deliberate about daily walking in it.

OR

- I am currently in a flip-flopping process where I am struggling most times with uncertainty about who I am. A lot of the things I use to define who I have nothing to do with God or the Bible. Apart from that, most other times I also struggle to believe who the Bible says I am.

2 ***What is my God-given purpose?***

- I know what God has called me to do, and I am actively preparing or currently engaged in walking out my purpose.

OR

- I have no idea what my purpose is, and I am mostly unsure if I am doing what God has called me to do.

3 ***How does the person (or type of persons) that I desire to date fit in with my God-given purpose?***

- Because I know my purpose, I am able to readily identify if a person I desire to date complements, detracts from, or even opposes my God-given purpose.

OR

- I have not considered how the potential date fits in; or I have seen some signs that this person might make it difficult for me to fulfil my God-given purpose if we were to get serious, especially to the point of marriage.

What is my purpose for dating or desiring to date?

- I have prayed and gotten confirmation from God that this is the right time, and season to date with the purpose of finding a Godly partner. A partner whom I can eventually have a Godly relationship with, marry and fulfil the role of being the wife or husband God has called me to be - all to the glory and honour of His name.

OR

- *Whoa!!!*
  Marriage? Come on now!
  Where'd that come from?
  Let's not get that serious...
  I just want to date for fun and explore a little. Maybe even have a "little relationship" with "some amount" of intimacy... *but possibly marriage*? Let's not think that far. That is a major jump-off right there talking about marriage! I have no intention or desire to marry now or anytime in the near future (between 1 and 6 years). I

don't think I'm "marriage-ready", nor am I even working towards being marriage-ready.

5 ***Am I spiritually, emotionally, mentally, physically, and financially ready for dating with the potential end result of marriage?***

- I have a strong and stable relationship with God. I have dealt (or I'm purposefully dealing) with the emotional issues that could pose a problem to maintaining a Godly relationship. Mentally and physically, I am at a place to not only date but enter into and sustain a Godly relationship and marriage - if dating were to lead to that. Financially, I'm already stable, or at least have a plan which I am actively pursuing towards that goal.

OR

- I am ready for the fun and companionship of dating.
  Marriage?
  Ummm... Not so much.
  There are still way too many areas in my life that need work before I will be ready to marry. Spiritually, I hardly have a clue about who I am called to be as a Christian and how to obey and submit to God's will for my life. Neither do I think that I have had sufficient life experiences to help mould and mature my mental and emotional capacity. Financially: I am not yet at a place of comfort or even have a plan towards that at the

moment, and even more, I have poor money management skills. Plus, I am still completely or heavily dependent on others to meet my financial needs.

You would realize by now that I keep hitting home the point of "*possibly leading to marriage*". For some persons, this might have made you uncomfortable, maybe even slightly annoyed that it keeps coming up.

However, I'll ask you this...

As a Christian, what is the point of dating if not to eventually culminate in marriage once the right partner is found?

Christians are not called to be "serial daters". And except for "serial daters", I don't know of anyone who dates in perpetuity. There must be an end goal in mind somewhere. For the Christian, what is that end goal if not marriage?

A serial dater is someone who dates for the "thrill" of dating without intentions of pursuing a settled relationship, or marriage.

Serial dating is of the world, **not of God.**

Think on this...

The world promotes dating (mostly inclusive of sex) which then progresses to either marriage, common-law union or breakups and then the cycle begins all over again. Let me ask then...

What do you expect of Christian dating?

Certainly not for persons to remain at the "getting to know each other" stage forever! If not, then wouldn't the expected natural progression eventually be "to marriage", once there is spiritual compatibility and physical and emotional attraction? This goes to show that Christian dating is not to be entered into unadvisedly or merely for fun and frolic. There has to be an end goal in mind, and it certainly shouldn't be a worldly one.

The questions outlined previously, are but the tip of the iceberg that Christians need to explore before deciding to date.

I leave you with this.

In case you may be thinking that the bar is set too high, consider diligently, what your motives are for dating, and how they line up with the Word of God. Are you seeking to date solely for your pleasure or for further alignment with God's purpose?

The world presents dating as an event of mostly frills and fun. One which is entered into at will and in fulfilment of self-motivated desires, inclusive of sex outside of marriage. While it is natural for Christians to be physically and sexually attracted to the opposite sex, we are called to live our lives by Godly principles. This includes bringing our bodies under subjection to the Word of God so that we do not engage in sexual immorality. Equally...

Many Christians desire to date and that is perfectly fine!

However, many might find that their "desire" to date is not synonymous with them being "ready" to date. Separate "desire" from "readiness". See where there are red flags and work on them.

Let your actions be "Spirit-led", not "flesh-forced."

Readiness trumps desire.

For Christians already in, or considering entering the dating pool, there are several guidelines to be considered both before and during. Chief of which is the answer to the question, *"Am I ready for dating - based on Biblical and practical guidelines?"* Christians are not of the world and so, the world's purpose and guidelines for dating should not be used as the benchmark for Christian dating. It therefore becomes important for Christian dating to be governed and regulated by Godly principles, as this will safeguard against the pursuit of "flesh-satisfaction" and sin.

In order to make decisions that are in line with the Word of God, Christians who are dating or considering dating need to be sufficiently armed with the truth. The truth has already been outlined in this chapter so as to assist you in identifying whether you are ready for dating. With your "state of readiness" already dealt with, let's now move on to the next chapter where we will look at the truth surrounding the motives and guidelines for Christian dating.

LET'S REFLECT!

Having read this chapter, what are some important points that you'd like to note?

Note to self...

"If you live by God's principles then you are His child. Equally, if you live by the world's standards and principles, then clearly, you belong to the world. As a Child of God, you can't date as the world does." #WhoAreYouFollowing

Kayon Rodney

GOD'S
WAY

CHAPTER 7

#RELATIONSHIP.GOALS

Motives & Guidelines for Christian Dating

As Christians, we should always be willing to assess our motives and desires against the Word of God. This is what will help us to separate flesh from Spirit and provide the Godly framework within which to operate. The same is true regarding the motives for dating or desiring to date. *Hold them up against the light of truth - The Word of God*

Oftentimes however, we deliberately choose not to assess our desires against the Word of God because we fear the truth would oppose what we have already purposed to do. So, regardless of whether it meets with God's approval or not, many prefer to hide behind ignorance.

Remember...

In Christendom, ignorance is most definitely not bliss.

Rather...

Knowledge is key!

FACING ME BEFORE DATING YOU...

Putting the horse before the cart...

Let us first deal with the ***"WHY"***, before we consider the ***"HOW"*** of Christian dating.

Do me this favour...

Look at yourself in the mirror and ask yourself this question:

Why would I want to date me?

Don't move! Stay right there!

Now, *respond to the question you just asked yourself.*

You see, simple and even foolish as this activity might seem, it is a valuable activity, and one which many persons might even find difficult to perform. This is so as all many will see are their broken selves staring back at them, while the enemy is in the background of their minds flinging accusations back and forth.

Several negative feelings may also begin to surface as an indication of unresolved issues surrounding their identities, such as unhealed traumas, insecurities, guilt, shame, accusations, betrayal, mistrust, unforgiveness (of self and others), broken self-esteem and so on. If you are such a person, even before we get further into assessing motives, this is an indication that you need to spend some more time with God and allow Him to bring healing before bringing another person into the mix. If not, you run the risk of bleeding over others and perpetuating a cycle of brokenness, as you expect others to provide the healing that you need.

Learn to "face" yourself before dating anyone...

Equally, there are others whose responses to the question might border on pride overload. They may list so many "perfect" attributes that one might be tempted into thinking that they have already attained all the perfecting that God promised would continue until Christ's return. If that's you, then...

Hey!

Get over yourself!

You're still a work in progress...

A mindset of "*cause I'm perfect*" or "*who wouldn't want to date me?*" is a recipe for disaster in any dating relationship. Persons with this prideful mindset tend to have unrealistic expectations of others. This often extends to expecting others to meet and live up to "their" standards, even over those as set by God.

Temper your pride...

Don't be like the Scribes and Pharisees by setting hifalutin standards for others, which even you yourself are incapable of living up to.

If however, your response was more balanced... maybe fitting somewhere along the lines of, because:

"God has been grooming and preparing me, such that my validation and completion is found in, and will always be from Him. I understand my individual purpose in life, even though I admit that I am still a work in progress. Further, this is what God desires for me in this season; to complement another person as chosen by Him, even as we both seek to fulfil God's will for our lives."

An answer along these lines indicates that you understand that without God you are nothing, that you need Him to make you complete for His purpose. In addition, it centres around God and seeking to please Him in all things, including dating for purpose and not for worldly pursuits and motives. A heart's posture as such shows both humility and an understanding of responsibility to purpose.

That being straightened out, let's further assess the various covert and overt motives for desiring to date.

<u>The world or the Word!</u>

MOTIVES FOR DATING

The following table should increase your knowledge by providing you with a side-by-side comparison of some of the motives surrounding dating. On one side there is the often prevailing "world" view and on the other is the Biblical response to what the world says. This should help you to assess your motives for dating. As you hold these views (and other views you will encounter elsewhere) against the Word of God, you should get a clearer picture of whether you are motivated by fleshly desires and guidelines set by the world, or those established by the Word of God.

Here's the truth:

Two roads before you, choose one.

The WORLD says... *I want to date because I want to:*	**The WORD responds...**
Find someone to love me.	✓ *"Greater love has no one than this, than to lay down one's life for his friends."* **John 15:13** ✓ *"But God demonstrates his own love for us in this: While we were still sinners, Christ died for us."* **Romans 5:8**
Have "relationship goal" moments.	✓ *"Flee also youthful lusts: but follow righteousness, faith, charity, peace, with them that call on the Lord out of a pure heart."* **2 Timothy 2:22-26**

Be able to have fun, sex and intimacy with someone. When you do these things, especially having sex before marriage it helps to determine compatibility.	✓ *"Flee sexual immorality! Every sin that a man does is outside the body, but he who commits sexual immorality sins against his own body."* **1 Corinthians 6:18** ✓ *"Don't you realize that your body is the temple of the Holy Spirit, who lives in you and was given to you by God? You do not belong to yourself,"* **1 Corinthians 6:19** ✓ *"For this is the will of God, your sanctification: that you abstain from sexual immorality; that each one of you know how to control his own body in holiness and honor, not in the passion of lust like the Gentiles who do not know God:"* **1 Thessalonians 4:3-5**
Find someone to complete me.	✓ *"And ye are complete in him, which is the head of all principality and power:"* **Colossians 2:10**
Find someone to ease my emotional, financial, and "other" burdens and needs.	✓ *"Cast thy burden upon the Lord, and he shall sustain thee: he shall never suffer the righteous to be moved."* **Psalm 55:22** ✓ *"Come to me, all you who are weary and burdened, and I will give you rest."* **Matthew 11:28** (NIV) ✓ *"And my God will supply every need of yours according to his riches in glory in Christ Jesus."* **Philippians 4:19**

Find someone to ease my loneliness and make me happy.	✓ *"You make known to me the path of life; in your presence there is fullness of joy; at your right hand are pleasures forevermore."* **Psalm 16:11** ✓ *"Until now you have asked nothing in My name. Ask, and you will receive, that your joy may be full."* ***John 16:24*** ✓ *"He that handleth a matter wisely shall find good: and whoso trusteth in the Lord, happy is he."* **Proverbs 16:20** ✓ *"Happy is that people, that is in such a case: yea, happy is that people, whose God is the Lord."* **Psalm 144:15**
Fit in. I feel like I'm missing out. Everyone else is dating or in a relationship, and I want to do it too. It doesn't matter. It is just for fun and testing the waters, nothing too serious.	✓ *"And do not be conformed to this world, but be transformed by the renewing of your mind, that you may prove what is that good and acceptable and perfect will of God."* **Romans 12:2**
Satisfy these sexual desires. They are so strong! I feel myself naturally being pulled in this direction, where I can date and also share sexual intimacy.	✓ *"No temptation has overtaken you that is not common to man. God is faithful, and he will not let you be tempted beyond your ability, but with the temptation he will also provide the way of escape, that you may be able to endure it."* **1 Corinthians 10:13**

As you assess the differing views, you quickly come to the realization that the similarity between the "world" and the "Word" view ends at the point where the two words sound alike. Aside from that, they are like oil and vinegar. They just do not mix.

Having assessed your readiness and motives, you should be in a better place to see whether you are going down the right or wrong path. Equally, be sensitive to the Holy Spirit's leading. He will surely be there guiding and convicting as you assess your dating readiness and motives.

So, what am I saying after allllll that?

Simply put, the world and the Word of God stand on opposing ends when it comes to the readiness for, ideals and purposes of dating. I am not here to promote or argue against dating, but rather, to provide you with Biblical truths which can help guide you into making the right decision as directed by the Word of God.

Therefore, if your readiness and motives for dating are not lining up with God's Word, then back to the drawing board! No need to rush. Work on you and your relationship with God first, before throwing another human into the mix.

> **If your readiness and motives are not lining up with God's Word, then back to the drawing board!**
>
> Work on you and your relationship with God first, before throwing another human into the mix.

And while I'm on this point...

For those who are single, learn to enjoy being single!

Matter of fact. Change the way you consider being single if it is an unfavourable view. Understand that *being single is not a curse! Neither is it a race to marriage.* No. Rather, *being single is a time of self-discovery and solidifying your relationship with God*. Focus on growing and maturing spiritually while you are single. You will surely need this strength to walk in your purpose and also for helping to maintain a Godly marriage; assuming that it is God's will for you to marry.

CHRISTIAN GUIDELINES FOR DATING

For those who would have considered all the factors above, among other things (chief of which is actively seeking God in fasting and prayer), and have come to the conclusion that indeed their readiness and motives are in line with the will of God, then here are some general pointers for dating:

✓ Aside from praying, fasting and asking God for clarity and guidance on who to date, consult your spiritual leaders. Most churches have protocols and guidelines which are followed whenever they have members who desire to date. This helps to provide spiritual guidance and some level of accountability as well. *If you find that you have a desire to hide and date, that is a red flag*, and also an open door for the enemy to step in and cause mischief. I encourage you to avoid this "hide and date" temptation at all costs.

✓ Do not rush. Get to know persons as friends before deciding whether or not to venture into the realm of dating.

✓ Do not go buying rings, dresses and tuxes just because you have a date. Not all dates will result in marriage. Pray, fast, observe, and evaluate the interests and purpose of your date against your interests and purpose in Christ.

✓ Dating is not synonymous with marriage and by virtue of this, **DOES NOT** qualify for the same rights, duties and privileges. For example, by God's standards, husbands and wives have the right, duty and privilege of having sexual intercourse within the sanctity of their union. Persons who are dating do not, that is fornication, which is a sin.

Dating is not synonymous with marriage

and
by virtue of this

DOES NOT qualify for the same rights, duties and privileges.

Equally...
Just to ensure there are no loopholes...

Aside from "sexual intercourse", there are several other sexually stimulating behaviours that Christians should avoid as they date. Deliberately engaging in sexually arousing behaviours outside of a marital union falls in the category of sin. That is allowing someone unapproved access to the Holy Spirit's temple – your body. There goes *petting* and *necking,* to name a few...

Right out the window!

✓ Find accountability partners in friends and counsellors. Those who will be able to offer spiritual support and guidance as well as help to hold you accountable to Godly principles as you date.

Just for the record...

Ensure that these are not persons who just automatically agree with everything you say, but are persons who will speak the truth even when it is unpopular, or painful to hear. The Bible tells us that, "*Faithful are the wounds of a friend, but the kisses of an enemy are deceitful*" **Proverbs 27:6**. Sometimes the wounds are what is needed, and not Band-Aids over potential sores.

✓ Carefully choose who to date. *Is your choice of a date pushing you into the realm of being unequally yoked with an unbeliever?*

✓ Make an assessment of your date's beliefs, intents and desires for dating. *Are they lining up with God's Word, or are they of the worldview? Do the things they encourage push you towards or away from God?*

✓ As you date you also need to make assessments about the spiritual, mental, and emotional maturity and readiness of the person you are dating. *How do they line up with where you are with God, and where you are going?* In addition, do not depend solely on the title "Christian" to decide if someone is spiritually aligned. Look at the fruit and lifestyle - as Christians are identifiable by their fruit, not title. *Are they demonstrating the Fruit of the Spirit?*

✓ *Remember those normal sexual desires I mentioned earlier?* You don't want to provide opportunities that increase them while diminishing your self-control. Therefore;

- **Be strategic in your choice of dating & meeting sites**. No use setting yourself up for unnecessary temptation. Avoid having dates in secluded places where the temptation becomes even greater. In other words, don't be tempted to test the waters, or see how far you can go before self-control runs out.
- **Exercise care in your speech and actions.** Do not seek to intentionally fuel your, or another's sexual desires as you date. The Bible warns in **Song of Solomon 2:7**, that you should not awaken love until the time is right (*paraphrase*). Many have fallen into sin by fulfilling sexual desires outside of marriage (including through masturbation), because they entertained speech and actions which fueled intense sexual arousal. So, avoid playing with temptations and sin. They don't ever play fair.

Keep it Godly and pure.

Find fun, appropriate things to do together as you get to know more about each other.

There are several spiritual and other factors that a Christian should consider before entering the dating pool. While the pointers above are helpful, they are by no means meant to be exhaustive. As with everything else, a Christian's life should be guided by the Word of God and maintaining a relationship with Him. This of course can only come from spending time in the Word, fasting and prayer. Do the same when it comes on to dating.

Invite God into the process.

You see, abiding by Godly principles (especially in this area and era) is not always seen as "fashionable". However, as Christians, we are not called to "seasonal righteousness" which changes with the season and location - as happens with fashion. The righteous requirements of God remain constant – whether you are in college or out, dating, thinking of dating, married, at home or on the street, in church or on a bus, in the Caribbean, Middle East, America, or Europe. I think you get the picture… Holiness to God in every area of our lives (including our bodies) is a lifestyle of **consistent** and **deliberate** choices governed by the Word.

Yes…

This also relates to:
choosing whether or not you are ready for dating,
who to date, how to date, boundaries and so on.

HIGHWAY HOPSCOTCH

The game of hopscotch comes to mind when one thinks of the worldly version of "dating" which occurs among many youths in college. I have witnessed firsthand the painful results of broken promises (and persons) which are the byproducts of ill-advised or many times "non" advised dating and casual relationships. Most of these dating relationships came about as a result of convenience and fleeting desires (lust), rather than purposeful and levelheaded God-guided plans. So, someone tickles a fancy and ignites the flesh and just like that...*whoosh...* off full speed on the "dating" highway. No consideration for warning signs or safety gears.

Though this happens with all year groups, it is especially most evident among the first-year (freshman) batches where there are several casualties on the "dating" highway. These often come about as inexperience and immaturity meet independence. Add to that, unabated freedom, fueled by experiments with worldly desires, and the results are crashing consequences with physical, spiritual and emotional damages. Damages which remain, as in this regard, what happens in college surely doesn't just "stay" in college. It often follows you throughout life, impacting your decisions and future relationships.

In college, many persons enter "relationships" and "fling-ships" for the immediate fun and excitement of it, with no real consideration of personal readiness, maturity or purpose. The euphoria rarely ever lasts however, and within a short period of time most of these "arrangements" fizzle out, leaving feelings of hurt, guilt and shame in their wake. Sometimes too, the grades of one or both parties suffer - both during and after these flings. Before long, unless persons find other worthwhile pursuits, they end up in other "entanglements" and the cycle continues.

Hopscotch!!!

Each time however, painful scars and baggage are added and the load gets heavier. This "load" doesn't just disappear after graduation either. Nope. These become unwanted emotional and spiritual baggage and scars from which persons will need to heal. So...

Don't be fooled!

What happens in college doesn't stay in college.

Here's the bottom line: God does not desire His children to be burdened by pain and hurt from ill-advised and oftentimes, rebellious decisions. Even as He provides guidance and wisdom through His Word, however, He also gives everyone free will. Free will to choose the path of righteousness or sin. It serves us well to always remember that, as Christians, we do not belong to ourselves but to God.

Though our bodies are made of flesh, they are more than flesh. Our body, is most importantly, the temple of the

Holy Spirit. Let Him be pleased to dwell there. Therefore, invite the Holy Spirit into your decisions as you explore your motives and readiness for dating, the Christian way. Do not be blindsided by the world and its overt and covert inducements to put self-gratification above the will and purposes of God.

LET'S REFLECT!

Having read this chapter, what are some important points that you'd like to note?

Note to self...

"Cultivate the right mindset: don't just settle for pursuing GPAs. Maximize your potential for the season you are in."

Kayon Rodney

POTENTIAL Loading...

CHAPTER 8

ACADEMIC SUCCESS: CULTIVATING THE RIGHT MINDSET

C*hange your focus!*

If you are looking for a 10-point plan to get you that 4.0 GPA (5.0 or even 13.0 in some countries), then, I'm sorry to disappoint you.

THIS IS NOT IT!

What this is, however, is a set of guidelines that will help you utilize Biblical principles to govern academic success while unearthing your greatest potential.

The *Oxford Learner's Dictionary* defines potential as, "*qualities that exist and can be developed.*" We are all born with innate abilities (the mental and physical capacity) to accomplish diverse tasks and achieve various goals.

However, it is our willingness to tap into those abilities and push them (and by extension, ourselves) to the ultimate limit, which determines whether or not we achieve our greatest potential. Our greatest potential, therefore, is not static and does not look the same for everyone, as we are all born with unique God-given abilities and strengths.

Examine the following diagram for an illustration of ability and potential in action, as displayed by two students, Liam and Alaina.

Did you get it?

Based on the illustration, both students are achieving the same grades on average. Liam is doing so using very little ability and is barely tapping into his potential. He has, however, chosen to settle with doing the "bare minimum" and operating below his potential, as he has "a good GPA" based on the standard set. Unfortunately, this mindset hinders him from walking into the best that God has for him in that season, as well as developing his natural abilities to their fullest.

Alaina on the other hand, is expending more effort and maximizing her natural abilities, thereby achieving the same GPA. She is not settling for anything less than her best, and even then, embraces opportunities for improving on what she has done. Alaina should therefore feel a greater sense of achievement as she is pushing her academic giftedness to greater dimensions and therefore, is well on her way to achieving her greatest potential in this regard. This is well-pleasing to God, as she is engaged in doing her best as unto Him.

Here's a kicker for you!

Based on a similar line of reasoning as above...

Someone with a 2.5 GPA, may be more aligned with purpose and achieving his or her fullest potential in that season, than another person who has, say, a 4.0 GPA.

Here's why...

Your fullest potential is not measured by your GPA; which is just one aspect of your life. Rather, attaining your greatest potential is a lifelong pursuit that is measured by your achieving the purpose for which God has called you for each season, and indeed life. A crucial element of this entails utilizing Godly principles in pursuit of purpose.

How do you do this?

Start by committing to and cultivating the right mindset.

MAXIMIZING YOUR POTENTIAL: THE RIGHT MINDSET

Maximizing your potential as a Christian in college requires that you identify and harness your God-given abilities, to produce the greatest results that you can achieve, through hard work, faith and perseverance. It is not merely settling for a man-made assessment of academic success, such as high GPAs. I want you to look beyond that mindset when we speak of success (including academic success). Many persons are "successful" by man's standards based on their attainments, but in actuality, are operating within the sphere of failure based on God's standards and assessment.

Many persons are "successful" by man's standards *but in actuality,* **are *operating within the sphere of failure based on God's standards and assessment.***

I love this line from "Mind Renewal", by Leostone Morrison, which puts it quite plainly: "*anything below your full potential is failure*". Therefore, even if you top the class by virtue of high academic performance, but are still doing less than the best that you can, then, you are not truly successful, you are just "settling".

> *Settling for doing better than others, but not living up to the best you can do.*

Note:

Don't let your determination of success become hinged on the performance of others (good or bad).

Let your success be defined by doing the best you can at all times in everything that you do, even as you leave the results up to God.

So, don't just settle for pursuing GPAs, maximize your potential for the season you are in. If it lands you a 4.0 or more, then great! If it lands you below the 4.0, then still great! *Why?* Because you would've maximized your potential and done your best.

Don't think I am downplaying a 4.0 GPA or trying to talk you out of pursuing one. *Absolutely not!* By all means, seek after good things, but here I show you an even more excellent pursuit. The pursuit of the right mindset for success academically and in all other areas. The kind of success which isn't determined by man's standards, but is a personal journey between you and God.

Aim to **maximize your potential** by doing the best you can in everything that you do.

Anything less is *"settling"*, and not true success.

So, yes...

A high GPA is absolutely awesome, but, pales in comparison to maximizing your potential. There are persons who limit themselves to settling for "appealing" GPAs, with no consideration for pursuing their best in all areas.

Here's the open secret, in case you missed it...

A 4.0 GPA does not indicate that you are walking in purpose or even your greatest potential. What it says, is that academically, you have earned an 'A' average in all of your classes or courses. While not taking away from this prestigious and often hard-earned accomplishment, for the Christian, "achievement" has to count for more than just high GPAs.

At the centre of it all is GOD. Seeking to please Him and becoming all that He intends for you to be in every season. As a Christian, my measure of success in college was not so much that I had a high GPA. Rather, it is that I look back and feel completely satisfied that in everything, I produced the best I could – given my abilities. This was achieved by identifying and tapping into my natural abilities through faith, obedience and extremely *HARD WORK*, while trusting God with the results.

This is a stark contrast to my attitude in high school. I was more like Liam in high school. It was never about doing my best, but rather, fulfilling the requirements (even barely) as set by the education system. In college, however, my drive was to give my best, as unto God.

I also understood from early in my college journey, that academic success was not going to be attained by a magic formula. Nor was it going to be attained by walking around all day with a big Bible in my hand, neglecting my academics, while telling others, "God is my Father, He will grant me success!" Oh no! That would be flawed thinking and action. *Yes, God is my Father, and yes, He is faithful,* but He is also a principled and practical God. He doesn't spoil His children or promote laziness and mediocrity. He gives His best and also expects us to give our best in all that we do.

Simply put, being in a relationship with God does not mean you get a free pass to reaping academic success without sowing hard work. If I wanted academic success and to maximize my potential in that season, I knew I'd have to put in the requisite hard work, even while ensuring my actions lined up with God's will.

That I did!!

So, here's the deal...

Purpose to pursue and maximize your potential based on your God-given abilities. Push them to the limit by doing the absolute best you can at all times in every academic pursuit. Do this with the understanding and attitude that God requires you to give of your best at all times, performing each task as doing it unto Him, and not merely for attaining standards as set by others. With this mindset, you will maximize your potential.

After all...

Would you be so presumptuous as to give God less than your best?

I leave you to answer that question.

Now that we have cultivated the right mindset regarding academic success, let's head on over to the next chapter, where I'll share with you some practical and Biblically grounded strategies that you can use in your pursuit of maximizing your academic potential.

LET'S REFLECT!

Having read this chapter, what are some important points that you'd like to note?

Note to self...

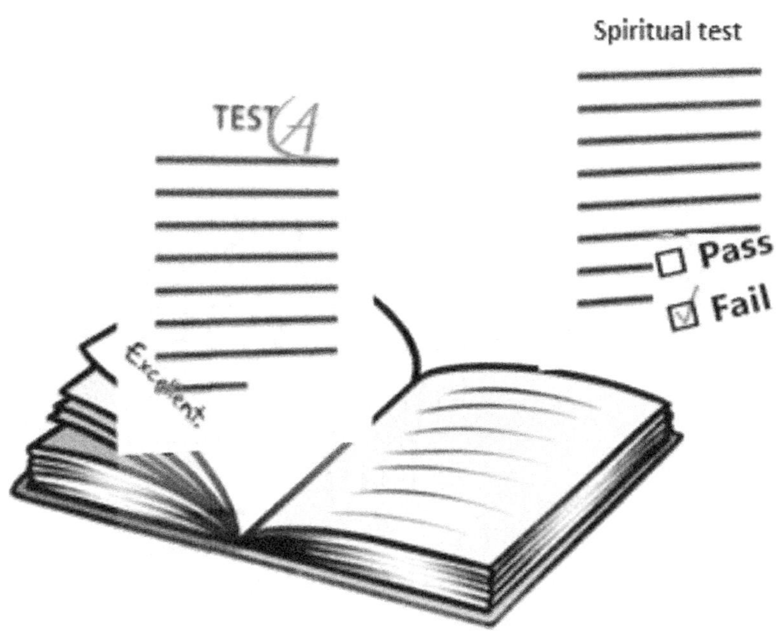

"Success is open to all. Success, God's way, however, is reserved for those who choose to follow His principles while maximizing their potential."

Kayon Rodney

God's way
attitude
success
natural abilities
laugh
take breaks
challenge
best
Potential
integrity
Maximize
organized

CHAPTER 9

PRINCIPLES FOR ACADEMIC SUCCESS: GOD'S WAY

Academic success is open to all.

Academic success, God's way, however, is reserved for those who choose to apply Godly principles in their lives, including their academics, while maximizing their potential.

The Godly route to academic success, however, challenges many in college, especially Christians. Often this is so as the demands to produce get pitched against heavy workloads, tight timeframes and alluring temptations to "settle" or compromise integrity. Yet, even with all these, it is possible to achieve academic success God's way. In fact, those "temptations" should push the Christian to greater dependence on God for His help to remain steadfast amidst the pressures. This by extension, helps to foster a deeper relationship with God as He helps you to navigate the potential snares on the academic journey.

I reiterate...

There are several ways to arrive at academic success, but not all are sanctioned by God. Those sanctioned by God are those that should be employed by Christians as they pursue academic success.

> *Ensure your academic success is not at the expense of spiritual compromise and failure. A passing grade or a "good GPA" is not worth failing the spiritual test.*

Remember, seek to please God in all areas of your life (including academics) as you pursue your greatest potential in the season you are in. As Christians, we pursue God and do our best in all things, trusting that GPAs will fall in line according to His will.

10 POINTERS FOR ACADEMIC SUCCESS: GOD'S WAY

> *It is possible to achieve academic success without compromising Godliness!*

Let me show you the basics.

What I am about to share with you are some of the Biblical principles and other strategies that I consistently applied in my academic pursuits throughout college as a Christian. Many of these principles have life-changing lessons, not just for academics, but for life in general.

1 ***Refuse to answer the calls from mediocrity.***

Remember I told you in a previous chapter about my arch-nemesis, mediocrity?

Yes, mediocrity…

Thankfully, this arch-nemesis is also not on friendly terms with my Father. In fact, God warns us against mediocrity. We find these instructions in various Bible verses. For example, **Ecclesiastes 9:10** tells us that, *"Whatever your hand finds to do, do it with your might…"*, and this is reiterated in **Colossians 3:23,** *"Whatever you do, work heartily, as for the Lord and not for men"*. These are only two of several verses which instruct us to do the best we can at all times.

> **If you live** your life **under** the shadow of **mediocrity**, **you will never realize the fullness of** what **God** has placed in you and ordained for you.
>
> *Purpose to* ***go beyond just scratching the surface!***

In college, and indeed life, however, mediocrity is always calling, using the line, *"Do just enough, and no more."* Refuse to answer that call. If you live your life under the shadow of mediocrity, you will never walk into the fullness that God has ordained for you. As I purposed in my heart and did then, I encourage you to so do; approach each assignment, each task with the intention of doing your best. Purpose to go beyond just scratching the surface, or settling for what others have done, or will do.

Is there a new dimension of creativity and expression that you can bring?

Do you know what the beauty is in all of this?

The Holy Spirit is always there with you, giving thoughts and ideas which you can try as you seek to do your best in all tasks. The challenge, however, is that oftentimes we ignore these thoughts by charting them down as being "*too hard*" or "*extra work*". At other times, we give in to fears of:

"*What if it doesn't turn out well?*

What if I'm wrong?

What if it's different from what others are doing?"

OK.

So what!!

It will either turn out to be a testimony or a lesson. Maybe both!

Stop allowing *"what ifs"* to keep holding you hostage, in fear of the unknown.

I mean...

Aren't you tired?

That's a good place to start. Become sick and tired of the *"what ifs"!* You have been giving them an audience for way too long. And a mind held hostage by fears of the unknown will always operate below its full potential. Therefore, starting right now, I encourage you, refuse to live any longer in the prison of negative "what-ifs". Break free by choosing to trust that all things will work for good, regardless of the process.

Why?

Well, simple really...

<u>YOU LOVE THE LORD AND ARE CALLED ACCORDING TO HIS PURPOSE!</u>

That describes you right?

2 ***<u>Dare to doubt your doubts!</u>***

Pray and work by faith. Trust God to guide you on the right path as you throw everything in you, behind each task or assignment. It might help you to realize that it's not just a "you" thing. Doubt and fear try to back all of us into corners. Not convinced?

Let me confess...

98% of the time I had no idea how to complete 99% of the assignments and tasks I had to do, even while doing them. I chose, however, to trust God above the fears and doubts.

I researched, networked, and put my best foot forward, following the creative and expressive thoughts that just kept coming at me throughout the process. Yes, it often took me into "harder" work than what many others chose to do, but I also ended up learning so much more. This knowledge wasn't limited to academics either, but I learnt more about who I am as a person, and more about my abilities and potential.

Yes, it requires hard work and perseverance, but hey... doesn't everything good that is worth having? I encourage you to work by faith and put your best into all tasks and assignments. It pleases God and pays off in more than just grades.

Identify and hone your natural abilities (strong points)

You would've realized certain characteristics about yourself by now, such as you are better at some things than others. The same goes for academics. One of the first things I would encourage you to do is try and identify any special skills that you might have, as well as how you learn best (your learning style).

Some persons are better able to grasp concepts when they hear them being spoken or sung (auditory learners), others when they view the information (visual learners), and there are also those who learn best by physically engaging in the task (tactile learners). You may find that you are able to learn in all these ways, however, one might be more dominant, or there is a combination of two or more.

Once you have identified your strong points, utilize them as much as possible while engaging in assignments and studying. This will facilitate greater retention and expression of what you have learned. Equally, once you have identified a weak area, take the content and work at it outside of class if you have to. Seek help from others and do independent research. Don't just overlook concepts because you have difficulty grasping them. Oftentimes your failure to understand one concept has a ripple effect in other areas. Therefore, do the best you can and resist the urge to shut yourself off from learning challenging content.

Me?

Well, I discovered my natural abilities and used them to my advantage. So, my dominant learning styles are auditory and visual. Realizing this, I used both as much as possible, in my attempt to grasp content. I am not a passive learner, so I always engage lecturers and peers in discussions about content. Once I have an understanding, then I would write most of the notes in my own words and style of writing or presenting. Which, much to my amusement, and the often weird looks of my peers, consists of several colour combinations and even drawings.

Yes... I even drew what I understood!

I developed my own style of taking notes, which would probably make many persons dizzy, but worked quite well for me. I used several different coloured pens while taking notes, and while time-consuming, this helped in the retention of the information. *Don't ask me how*, it somehow worked for me and I utilized it, even without fully understanding the science behind it.

In addition, I am usually commended for my writing skills and style, so I also knew this was one of my strong points. Therefore, even if I could find content created by other persons, I would often challenge myself by creating original content for select assignments, which would even more aptly suit the need. This helped to develop my overall creativity, comprehension and writing skills.

Whenever I encountered weak areas, I would take the content and engage in personal research, finding videos, visuals and written content about the topic or concept. This facilitated seeing the content presented in many different ways and styles than just the one which might have been used in the lecture, and further added to my understanding. Equally, I would seek assistance from persons (including peers) who were more knowledgeable in the area. Whatever work needed to be put in, I would attempt to do so, never neglecting at all times to pray and ask God to increase my understanding throughout. God gives us wisdom for a reason. We just have to learn to apply it in all areas: spiritually, mentally, emotionally, financially, physically, academically, and so on.

4 ***Be organized***

Being organized is a must if you are going to see the greatest results! This means you must set goals and deadlines and try to stick to them. College is a hustle and bustle environment, and on any given day there are a million and one things to be done, in addition to preparation for other tasks and assignments which will be happening another day.

There is never a dull moment.

Being organized provides you with a comprehensive view of the upcoming tasks and assignments, so you are able to plan and execute effectively. This also ensures you are able to give each task your best effort as you work at them over time, rather than rushing to complete assignments that you only "just remembered" at the last minute – just before it's due. You are more likely to submit mediocre work when you are under pressure and strapped for time. Doing last-minute "touch-ups" on assignments is different from doing your assignment last minute.

How did I do it? Well...

Personally, I remained organized by using a Microsoft Excel spreadsheet to keep track of assignments and tasks. Each time I got the due date for a new task or assignment, I would input this information. Tasks were arranged by order of their due dates, with the assignments due soonest being closer to the top.

I also used simple colour coding to help keep track of what was complete (green) and what needed to be completed (red). While this was my strategy, some of my classmates used physical means, such as a dedicated assignment book. At intervals, we would also remind each other of upcoming assignments and whether due dates and requirements had been adjusted, and so on. While this is not necessarily the norm for all college mates, thankfully, my peers and I had a great support system in each other, thus staying organized was made even easier.

5 ***Take recreational breaks***

There's a saying which goes "all work and no play makes Jack a dull boy". I would hasten to add to that, "and Jill an even duller girl". That being said, being a Christian in college doesn't mean all academics and no fun. That's a recipe for burnout and failure. Part of maintaining academic success requires that you take recreational breaks to socialize with others, as well as take some "me" time.

This is an absolute must!

Take a break from the books!

Watch a movie, go to the park, go to the beach, go get ice cream, watch some cartoons, gather with peers, laugh... Whatever appropriate activity that brings you joy. This helps to reduce stress, improves memory and creativity, as well as boosts your energy. Take breaks in between completing assignments and as much as necessary. Whenever you are off on longer breaks, go visit family and friends. Catch up with old friends. Whatever you do, get some "you" time away from the books.

Align yourself with those you can both teach and learn from

The preference in college is always to align with those who are seen as "leaders" or "bright", those who we can learn from – especially for group assignments. While there is nothing wrong with drawing close to those with admirable qualities, consistently being on the "receiving end" however, also has the pitfall of limiting your own potential. This is so as you run the risk of becoming overly dependent on others and not spending enough time to identify and hone your special skills. One way to avoid this is by balancing your associations (especially for group work) with both those you can learn from and those you can teach.

As you learn from others, implement the admirable characteristics, along with your strengths and take on group members who can learn something from you. This has the dual benefit of helping others while developing your own skills and potential.

Here's another piece of valuable advice...

Actively participate in group discussions and group work. Do not be lacklustre and mediocre, while hoping that others will pick up the slack. *That is an unfair and ungodly attitude.* Further, active participation is a powerful strategy for content clarification and retention, which is facilitated as you "pull your weight" in group work and discussions.

Adjust your attitude to achieve the greatest altitude

If there ever was a lesson I learnt well, it was this one: *your attitude has an impact on your altitude*. The only grade I ever got in a college credit course, which was lower than "A", was the B+ that I scored in Music. God used this to teach me a lesson in "attitude adjustment".

So, our music course was split into two parts which would combine later into one grade for the entire course. In part A, the theoretical aspect, I disliked the course and all the musical terms and notes that I had to learn, but I bent my mind to the task, and did the best I could, earning an admirable grade.

However, by part B of the course the next semester, things took a turn for the worse. If I disliked part A, then I thoroughly abhorred part B. It was mostly practical, and I am not all that kinesthetically inclined. In other words, I am least adept at using my body as part of learning and completing tasks which require excessive coordinated movements.

In part B of this music course, a major part of the grade was for learning to play the recorder. You see my dilemma?

Oh, of all the dreadful tasks!

I hated the instrument with every fibre of my being!

Unfortunately, that was also the attitude I took to learning to play it. In my, albeit, weak defense, except for maybe two of my classmates, we all hated learning to play this instrument.

Needless to say, I got easily annoyed with learning to play the recorder. My fingers would be going in one direction, the tune in the other, and they rarely ever met for the beautiful symphony that was needed. It was like they hated each other or something. To make it worse, my intense dislike for this instrument was also affecting my interest and output.

No matter how I tried, I could never play beautifully, or even "slightly cute".

Not even close!

I was so over this recorder!

When the time came for the internal oral exam, I took that same annoyed and hateful attitude into the room. Oh how I played my frustration into each note! When I was finished massacring the tune and assaulting my lecturer's ears with my playing, I stated matter of factly, "*That's it!*" I left the exam room upset with the recorder, but moreso, myself for not having mastered it. Either way, I hoped that was the last I'd see of the wretched thing.

Fast forward to a few weeks later...

As fate would have it, a few persons were selected to be externally assessed on playing the recorder.

Guess who was one of the lucky ones chosen?

You guessed right! Me!

Oh, joy...

It most certainly wasn't because I had played beautifully! So, it had to have been that bad...

What to do?

I mean, what could I do?

I needed to pass this course in order to get my degree.

So, time to face the wretched recorder again. I did the only thing I could. I took the turn of events in stride. However, something happened that changed the whole trajectory of events.

It so happened that a few days after getting the news of my upcoming "external assessment", I had a chance encounter with my lecturer who had conducted the internal music assessment.

Well, I thought it was a chance encounter at the time. Now I realize it was ordained...

After exchanging pleasantries, and reiterating the fact that I was going to be one of those externally assessed; amidst my complaints, she gently touched my arm, smiled sweetly and said,

"Kayon, change your attitude."

Ms. Hoilett is a pretty small lady, but that day her voice echoed in my mind as if it came from a giant. If she had slapped me, I wouldn't have felt it as much.

Conviction sure does pack a punch!

Those four words hit home hard because immediately I felt convicted about the attitude I had taken toward learning to play the recorder.

This was it!

God used her words to get my attention.

It was time to face the music.

No pun intended...

One thing about being chastened by the Lord (in whatever way He chooses), it sure hits where it hurts. And He most certainly will not change His standards whether you choose to respond by bellyaching or rebelling. I was well acquainted with this fact, so falling in line it was! No bellyaching or rebelling.

So, for the next few weeks until the external assessment, I had an attitude overhaul. I kept practicing as much as I could. Even with all the mistakes, I stopped getting annoyed and took them in stride; stopping at intervals to tell God:

"Lord, here are my hands, fingers and the recorder. Help me to get it done."

Well, that He did...

I was externally assessed and did much better than the first time around. I'd love to say I played "beautifully", like an angel, but that would be far from the truth. My playing was still not beautiful and seamless, but it was much better and sufficed for me to get a better grade, even eventually copping the top prize for having the highest grade in the overall music course.

Like seriously, God?

Sometimes I think God has mighty strange methods of getting His messages across...

Top prize...

I mean, my playing certainly wasn't perfect, but it wasn't really about my playing so much. It was about teaching me the lesson of maintaining the right attitude in all things. A lesson that I would also need to share with others. Not only did I do my best on the second try, but this time I maintained the right attitude. That was well-pleasing to God. That was what He desired and He wouldn't let me off the hook. He needed me to get it right and I did.

Oh, the chastening of The Father for those whom He loves...

Lest I forget this lesson however, (even though I was awarded the prize for the highest grade) I scored a B+, missing the "A" by one mark. *One mark!* A mark that I could have easily gotten had I approached the course with the right attitude the first time around.

That B+ is my constant reminder that it is not so much that tasks might be challenging or situations are less than ideal; it is moreso the attitude that we employ as we go about these tasks that makes the difference. Further...

Talk about being presumptuous...

Here I was again!

It was part of God's will for me to take this course as I read for my degree, so I should've allowed Him to lead in all things instead of allowing my dislikes to rule my actions. In this case, this less than "perfect" grade encapsulated another lesson that I needed to learn; that of *maintaining the right attitude regardless of the circumstances.*

When we take the wrong attitude, we often speak and act out of turn, neglecting to do whatever we are tasked to do, as unto God. This goes contrary to God's instructions. Taking the wrong attitude also erects a mental block, and makes it difficult to operate at our full potential as we are blindsided by our negative perceptions. So here's my advice: be careful of the attitude you take towards your academics or specific areas or courses, as negative attitudes can negatively impact how well you perform.

P.S.

Yes, I learnt my lesson.

But...

IF I NEVER HOLD ANOTHER RECORDER, I CAN'T SAY THAT I WOULD BE SAD...

8 ***Maintain the highest level of (academic) integrity***

What would your reaction be, if, after all your hard work, another student took your paper and submitted it as his or her work?

You'd be mad as a hornet right?

Sadly, that right there, happens quite often in college. While it doesn't always involve an entire paper, many students, including Christians, are guilty of plagiarism –

taking other people's work, parts of their work, or ideas, and submitting it as their own.

The Bible tells us in **Isaiah 61:8**, that God loves justice, but hates robbery and wrong. Plagiarism is both robbery and wrong. To avoid plagiarism, be sure to learn how to properly give credit to persons whose work you have used as you researched for your assignment. This is usually taught as a foundational course in college.

Pay attention!

Sadly, however, this is one of the courses that many students take for granted, only to later realize the detriment of this mistake, as they run afoul of the requirements for academic integrity.

Plagiarism is a serious matter with ethical and legal implications. It certainly would be unfortunate to attend college to gain a degree and, instead, end up leaving with a blot on your character, and even your record, as a result of plagiarism. In the worst-case scenario, you could even be forced to leave college without a degree. Make wise choices. If in doubt or need clarity about possible issues of plagiarism, consult the librarian or a lecturer with the requisite knowledge prior to submitting your work.

Maintaining integrity is not just for assignments either. As Christians, we are also called to maintain integrity and honesty in our conduct in and out of the academic setting. So, for example, no matter how strapped you are for time, resist the temptation to just make up a little lie to get an extension for your assignment from the lecturer. Maintain your Godly integrity and character at all costs.

Do not hide from those who challenge you to produce "greater"

If ever there was a lecturer that I loved, but also would have loved to many times hide from (under a rock, space or anywhere she couldn't locate me), it was Mrs. Clayton-Johnson. She was my lecturer in all my science-related courses. She was a woman of faith, as well as one who sought to squeeze every drop of potential she could from ALL her students.

Remember I told you that I always tried to do my best in all things?

Well, in her courses, she wanted more than my best and was always pushing and prodding me for more. In fact, she did this with all of her students. I often wondered where she expected me to get this "*more*" from. It's not like I had a secret "stash" lying around somewhere in a safe or something. I already thought I was doing my best. I remember having a discussion with her once, and her telling me that because I exhibited such great potential, more was required of me. It was not that what I was producing was not good or would not land me a good grade, she just wanted the greatest I could produce, and she was not always convinced my first tries were such.

Her "squeezing" me for greater would many times leave me on the brink of tears as I had already worked so hard on the first and second drafts and had several other assignments (from other courses) working on at the same time, which were also due. Nevertheless, I would go back to the drawing board and dig even deeper, implementing her suggestions and allowing research and creativity to pull me into other areas. Many times, the "final" result was better than what was initially submitted to her, which I previously thought was my best. Demanding as those times were, they taught me that it is good to have persons who challenge us to dig deeper. This helps us to unveil hidden potential that we might not readily see on our own.

So, as tempting as it might be, if there is that one lecturer, group leader, or indeed person, who is just always pushing you to produce more, don't hide. Take little breaks from them if it gets overwhelming sometimes, but don't shy away from reaching for more. Sometimes they are seeing potential in you that you have not yet realized, and even "your best" can be improved upon. Be open to the challenge.

10 ***Labour on and give birth***

There will be many times on the journey that you feel like giving up. Times when you feel stretched beyond your limit and only the grace of God keeps you going. In times like these, don't despair, the period will pass. Keep on working at all that you have to do, one word, one sentence, one paragraph at a time. God did not bring you this far to leave you. Trust God, and keep putting in the work. He will sustain you.

There were many times that I too felt as if it was all too much. So many challenging assignments to complete, exams to prepare for, classes to catch, meetings to attend and deadlines to meet that it was beginning to seem like a blur. And that was just academics. Yet I persevered, like so many other persons in college and held on to my faith in God, and He brought about success.

So I encourage you, no matter how challenging it gets, choose to believe that God will take you through successfully. Just as with the labour process in childbirth, it will eventually come to an end, and your greatest potential would have been birthed.

The challenges of the college season are not forever.

They will pass!

Hang in there and push forward by faith, doing the best you can at all times while leaving the rest up to God. Even in the challenging times, remember to maintain Godly principles, understanding that your posture doesn't just reflect you, but your belief about the God you serve. Choose to trust God above it all, and be an example of a Believer who others can look up to.

In closing off this leg of our journey, I leave you with this reminder...

Success in college for Christians should be more than just the pursuit of admirable grades and a high GPA. Rather, it should be a holistic process of cultivating and maintaining Godly principles in all your pursuits, while allowing the process to unearth your full potential for that season. In some cases (dependent on several factors), this might result in a high GPA. In other cases, it might just result in a "pass". Whatever, the outcome, keep doing the best you can and trust that God will do the rest.

LET'S REFLECT!

Having read this chapter, what are some important points that you'd like to note?

Note to self...

EPILOGUE

The college period can be a wonderful time of growth and success. This however, requires that one cultivate and maintain the right attitudes, mindset and by extension actions. This is the difference between "*success in college*" and "*success in college – God's way*".

Pivotal to Godly success in college are practical endeavours such as learning to effectively handle stress, being both book and street savvy, even while maintaining Godly principles in all academic and social pursuits. The college period also provides the perfect opportunity for identifying and maximizing your greatest potential while charting a course for the rest of your life. However, there are many obstacles.

Obstacles in college come in various forms. For example, pressures and ungodly distractions which can promote spiritual stagnation and compromise. Even with the myriad of challenges and temptations, however, it is possible to achieve academic success without sacrificing your relationship with God. This requires that you be intentional in how you approach every aspect of the college experience. After all, *what happens in college does not stay in college* but has ripple effects in all areas of your life going forward. Decide what kind of ripples you want to have precede you.

Grab your copy of:

God goes to College too

Volume 1

Sneak peek of some topics in volume 1:

- Identity in ~~Crisis~~ Christ
- Introduction to self, others and purpose
- Kingdom keys for unlocking spiritual growth in college
- The training ground
- Being salt and light in college

ABOUT THE AUTHOR

Kayon Rodney is an educator by calling and training. She holds a Bachelor's degree in early childhood education, with first-class honours, and is the author of several Christian-based literature geared at imparting spiritual values and principles to children and youth, for whom she has a fierce passion.

As a member of the Victory Family Centre Church, she serves as the minister with responsibility for Children's Ministry, as well as on the team of teachers for the adults Sunday school. She is a dedicated wife and mother.

Made in the USA
Columbia, SC
08 March 2024

32905030R00114